AMELIA
EARHART

DARING WOMEN OF HISTORY

AMELIA EARHART

MIKE ROUSSEL

The History Press

Cover illustration courtesy of Mary S. Lovell

First published 2017

The History Press
The Mill, Brimscombe Port
Stroud, Gloucestershire, GL5 2QG
www.thehistorypress.co.uk

British Library Cataloguing in Publication Data.
A catalogue record for this book is available from the British Library.

ISBN 978 0 7509 7948 1

Typesetting and origination by The History Press
Printed and bound by CPI Group (UK) Ltd

CONTENTS

FOREWORD

BY JOY LOFTHOUSE
ATA PILOT 1943–45

As a young teenager, I marvelled at the flying achievements of Amelia Earhart and our own Amy Johnson. Of course, there was no television in the 1930s, but they often featured on the newsreels at cinemas.

At that time I could never have imagined that I myself would be flying during the Second World War. I was not a pre-war flier, but I was trained to fly as an Air Transport Auxiliary (ATA) ab initio pilot, so I was not in the ATA when the first American girls were brought over by Jacqueline Cochran. When America came into the war, most of these girls returned to serve in the Women Airforce Service Pilots (WASP). Of the few who stayed, I knew both Roberta Leveux and Ann Wood.

Despite the thrill of flying service aircraft for two years, the achievement of women such as Amelia Earhart, who flew such long distances, never ceased to enthral me, and this book is a tribute to a brave and bold woman who was ahead of her time in her daring and who inspired young women all over the world to 'have a go'.

ACKNOWLEDGEMENTS

My special thanks go to Joy Lofthouse for writing the foreword to this book. Joy's story can be read in *Spitfire's Forgotten Designer: The Career of Supermarine's Joe Smith*, published by The History Press.

I am indebted to all who gave me their support, advice and their time while I was researching this book, and also those who have loaned me photographs and other illustrations from their collections. These include Ron Dupas's 1000aircraftphotos.com, which includes photographs from the Jim Brink and Ed Garber Collection and David Horn Collection. Other photographs come from Bill Larkins, Jim Geldart, Grace McGuire, Mike Pocock, National Archives and Ames Historical Society Collection.

I am deeply indebted to Mary S. Lovell for the use of her research papers and photographs gathered in the process of writing her book, *The Sound of Wings*.

My grateful thanks go to Amy Rigg and her team at The History Press for their valuable professional advice and support through to the publication of my book.

I would also like to thank all I have contacted through their respective websites around the world for their help and support.

My special thanks go, as always, to my wife, Kay, for her constant support and encouragement of my work, and for keeping me refreshed with sandwiches and cups of coffee.

Whilst I have consistently aimed for accuracy and have contacted copyright owners where applicable, I can only apologise and stress that should there be any omission, please contact me through the publishers and it will be rectified in future editions.

INTRODUCTION

Amelia Earhart was suddenly catapulted into fame in 1928 when she became the first woman to fly across the Atlantic. She made the trip in the *Friendship* with Wilmer 'Bill' Shultz, the pilot, and Louis Gordon, the flight engineer. Amelia, a social worker at the time, had already learned to fly independently, and whenever she could manage it, she would go to the local airfield to increase her flying hours. The prospect of the Atlantic trip was an experience that she did not want to miss and her understanding manager at Denison House in Boston, Massachusetts, gave her time off so she could make the flight. Nonetheless, Amelia loved her work as a social worker teaching English to immigrant children, and planned to return to the role after the flight.

After the trip Amelia found herself at the centre of a media firestorm, but she was uncomfortable with the attention, feeling the celebrity status that was heaped upon her was misplaced because she did not actually do any of the flying herself; she was merely a passenger and commented that she felt 'like a sack of potatoes'. Despite trying to share the praise with the pilot and engineer, she was unsuccessful and they tended to be left in the background, at least in the UK. However, when the three aviators arrived back in the USA all this changed and the

Amelia enjoyed horse riding and rode regularly at Rye when she was at home. (Courtesy of Mary S. Lovell)

Standing in front of the PCA-2 Pitcairn autogiro. (Courtesy of Mary S. Lovell)

three of them were involved in the welcoming ticker tape parades. After this life-changing experience, Amelia vowed that she wanted to be the first woman to fly solo across the Atlantic, just as Charles Lindbergh had been the first man to do so in 1927.

Over the next few years Amelia was to become the best-known aviatrix in America, but much of the success in publicising her name must be attributed to the publisher George Putnam, who later became her husband. Her reputation became one of great daring and of a fierce determination to break records and push new boundaries in aviation. She was well known for her charismatic personality and outspoken nature, but the media quickly picked up on the remarkable coincidence that she physically resembled Charles Lindbergh. Charles was nicknamed 'Lucky Lindy', so they referred to Amelia as 'Lady Lindy'.

Amelia was born into the late Victorian era and would have been expected to settle into the traditional role of a young lady, but she would never have been content with that. She enjoyed spending her childhood years as a tomboy, along with her sister Muriel, and decided at an early age to do something about the male-dominated workplace, as she believed that women should have equal rights to men. As a child Amelia led a very peripatetic life, moving around with her father's work and attending many different schools. She was an intelligent, hard-working scholar and did not waste her time, something which did little to endear her to those of her peers who just wanted to fool around.

While at finishing school, she went to stay with her sister in Canada for the Christmas vacation, but after seeing the wounded Canadian military from the First World War she decided to stay and become a voluntary nurse working in the Spadina military hospital. Amelia discovered that some of the patients she nursed were pilots who had fought in the war and during her time at the hospital she got to know them quite well, sharing with them her interest in flying. When they had recovered enough they invited her to go with them to a local military airfield where she could watch the take-offs and landings. This reignited the interest that sparked after her first experience in a biplane, when her father paid for her to have a ten-minute flight with ex-army pilot Frank Hawks.

Amelia eventually took up flying lessons and bought her own plane, but was forced to take a series of jobs to help pay for it. After a time, she went to work at Denison House, and it was while working there that she was invited to take part in the *Friendship* flight. From that moment her flying career started to take off, with her breaking flying records, writing her first book about the *Friendship* flight and penning articles for magazines. She took part in lecture tours, became a career adviser to female students and even promoted her own fashion line, as well as endorsing various commercial products. Amelia's fame spread far and wide; soon it was not only in America that she was well known, but also around the world.

On 2 July 1937, Amelia, along with her navigator, Fred Noonan, disappeared without trace while making for a landing on the tiny Howland Island in the South Pacific. There have been many theories about what may have happened, but as yet no solid evidence has been produced.

1

TOMBOY YEARS

Amelia Earhart's story begins when her parents, Amy Otis and Edwin Earhart, met at a coming out ball. They were immediately attracted to one another, despite coming from entirely different backgrounds. Amy was born into a wealthy family, highly respected in their community, but Edwin had a less privileged upbringing. His father was a Lutheran minister and his family life was one of struggle and poverty. However, Edwin wanted to better his chances in life and worked hard to pay for his training as a lawyer at Kansas University.

Amy's father, Judge Alfred Otis, a retired district judge who, during his retirement, held positions as president of Atchison Savings Bank and warden of the Trinity Episcopal Church, was not entirely happy with the developing relationship between his daughter and Edwin. He did not consider her suitor to have a high enough social standing, but Judge Otis's concerns had no effect on Amy, who was deeply in love with this handsome and charming young man. Nonetheless, he was not convinced that Edwin, an inexperienced lawyer, would be able to achieve a salary sufficient to provide for his daughter's needs, so he set him a challenge: if

Amelia's parents, Edwin and Amy. (Courtesy of Mary S. Lovell)

he could achieve a salary of at least $50 a month, which he considered would be enough to provide for his daughter, then he would agree to give her hand in marriage. Edwin was determined to meet the challenge, but it took him five years to do it, during which time he worked as a claims lawyer for a railroad company. Throughout this time Edwin and Amy remained very much in love. They eventually married on 18 October 1895 at Trinity Episcopal Church in Atchison and lived in a fully furnished house in Kansas City, where Edwin worked, provided by Amy's parents.

Amelia Mary Earhart was born on 24 July 1897 at the home of her maternal grandparents in Atchison, Kansas. Amy had travelled there from Kansas City so that she could give birth to her baby where she had the support of her family and friends. The baby's names were chosen from both her grandmothers – Amelia Otis and Mary Earhart. Amelia's sister, Muriel, was born on 29 December 1899. As the sisters grew up they became very close and gave each other nicknames: 'Millie' for Amelia and 'Pidge' for Muriel.

Amelia's grandparents' house, where she was born. (Courtesy of Mary S. Lovell)

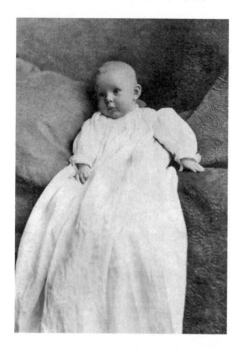

Amelia in her christening robe, October 1897. (Courtesy of Mary S. Lovell)

Amy did not find the deprivations of her married life easy, but was determined to do her best. However, it was soon apparent that Edwin was not good with money and found it difficult to provide for his family. This became a deep concern for Amy, who was struggling with the day-to-day needs of the family. Judge Otis also became very worried about his daughter, as it appeared that his initial misgivings might have been well founded.

Edwin wanted to prove himself and tried various plans to gain extra money. One was an invention for a signal flag holder for trains, for which he used the funds Amy had been saving to pay a tax bill, but he found that someone else had already patented a similar device. Judge Otis thought that the cost of the patent application and travel to Washington was a total waste of money.

Millie (Amelia) and Pidge (Muriel) sitting on the front porch at their Kansas City home, 1904. (Courtesy of Mary S. Lovell)

Nonetheless, Amelia spent her early years in some comfort, living with her grandparents during the winter months while studying at the same private college preparatory school that her mother had attended and returning to Kansas City for the holidays. Amelia's childhood was happy and she had family and friends all around her. The main conflict in her life was the expectation of her grandparents that she should behave in a more ladylike fashion, as per the social standards of the day, but she was more interested in adventure.

Amelia was known to be independent, clever and daring in the adventures and games she organised for her friends. She liked all types of sport and games, including riding bicycles and playing tennis and basketball. Amelia and Muriel's father was happy to see his daughters playing 'boys' games' and readily indulged them with footballs and sleds. In those days, girls were expected to ride short sledges while sitting upright, whereas boys had longer sledges on which they would lay face down and speed down the slopes. However, it was fortunate for Amelia that one Christmas her father gave her one of the longer sledges because it saved her from a serious accident. Amelia remembered speeding down a steep slope just as a rag-and-bone man with his horse and cart started to cross her path from a side road. There was no chance that she could turn the sled in time and fortunately it went between the front and back legs of the horse. Had she been sitting up on a short sled in the traditional way for girls her head would have struck the horse's ribs, causing her serious injury. This piece of good fortune did little to assuage the concerns of her maternal grandparents about the suitability of the girls' outdoor activities.

Amelia's mother was aware of the games the girls were involved in and had gym suits made up with bloomers gathered in at the knees, contrary to the conventional dresses that 'nice girls' were expected to wear. As a young lady, Amy had also taken part in adventurous activities and was the first woman to climb Pike's Peak, Colorado, so she was not overly concerned that both her daughters were similarly inclined.

Edwin was keen to ensure his family enjoyed the interesting experiences the world had to offer and spent hundreds of dollars taking them to the 1904 World's Fair in St Louis. Again, Judge Otis was not impressed, considering it to be yet another waste of money. Despite this, the girls had a wonderful time, so much so that Amelia, impressed by the roller coaster, built her own model version at her grandparents' home after their return. Yet again, her grandparents did not approve; they thought it highly dangerous and, as soon as her mother found out about it, Amelia was told to dismantle it.

In 1905 Edwin joined the claims department of the Rock Island Railroad Line. At last, with a regular salary, he was going to be able to make life more comfortable for the family, something they sorely needed, but it would mean another move, this time to Des Moines, Iowa.

While their parents were looking for a new home, the girls were left with their grandparents until a house could be arranged, but the anticipated stay of a few weeks took much longer than expected. Therefore, their grandparents, keen to encourage their educational development, arranged for the girls to attend a small private college preparatory school. Amelia enjoyed learning and developed a keen interest in all educational subjects, especially music, reading, writing, French, sewing, and, of course, sports. Although the girls missed their parents, living in their grandparents' home was comfortable and the couple were very pleased to have them. The girls also had two cousins who lived nearby, who they played with frequently.

In 1908 Amelia and Muriel joined their parents in Des Moines, but even while there the family still moved to four different homes. Their father travelled frequently for his work and the family often went with him. Happy summer holidays were spent at Worthington, on the shores of Lake Okabena. Edwin would take the girls fishing on the lake and Amelia played plenty of sports. She even learned to ride a 12-year-old Indian pony that belonged to some friends. Amelia said the pony 'could be bribed by cookies to do anything', and as there was no saddle available the sisters would ride it bareback. Amelia saw her first aeroplane at the 1908 Iowa State Fair at Des Moines. Interestingly, at the time it held no interest for her and she later commented that 'it was a thing of rusty wire and wood'.

In 1909, Edwin was promoted again, to claims agent. He was now in charge of a department and saw his salary almost double, plus he had the opportunity to use his own private railroad car for business and private use, which afforded Amelia the opportunity to travel to different parts of the country. She did not consider that her many trips away caused any detriment to her education, saying, 'It did not materially hinder school experience. I think possibly I gained as much from travel as from curricula.' This was also the opinion of her father, who would encourage his family to travel with him. Amy, who had for so long been burdened with the running of the household while trying to balance the diminishing finances, found that with her husband's promotion and increase in salary she was now in a position to employ staff to help her.

Life with their father had been far from dull and the girls had fond memories of the fun they had when he fooled around and played with them. Edwin read stories to them and would challenge them to tell him the meaning of strange words, some taken from a dictionary and some that he made up. More interestingly, he told them his own imaginary stories, mainly westerns, which Amelia said 'went on for weeks', with her father playing the leading role. At weekends he would join in with the girls and their friends, playing 'Chief Indian', with the scenes of the Indian wars re-enacted in their barn in Des Moines. One controversial thing Edwin did, which horrified Amelia's grandparents, was to give 9-year-old Amelia a .22 rifle to clear the barn of rats. Amelia had heard stories of the plague where the rats carried the disease around and was anxious that this should not happen to her family, but her grandparents thought a rifle was far too dangerous for a child of that age to use.

Family life was happy, but this was not to continue. As time went on their father started drinking heavily. The seriousness of his drinking habits became more of a problem when he started to do it during and after work, staying out late and imbibing with his friends. He would often arrive home late, much to the disappointment of the girls, who had been waiting for him to play with them. The girls started to call their father's alcoholism 'Dad's sickness'.

Edwin was warned by his employers that if he did not try to tackle his problem he would be fired. He sought medical help and was in hospital for a month, but on returning to work he started drinking again and this led to his dismissal. There was to be no more comfortable life and their mother had to work hard to keep things together, although Amelia, a resourceful girl, tried to help her mother where she could.

Amy's mother died on 21 February 1912 and her father just a few months later, on 9 May, leaving a substantial amount of money to be shared among their four children. Judge Otis had become more and more concerned about Edwin's drinking habits and the lack of provision he had made for his family. Amelia Otis had come to the same conclusion and so, to ensure Edwin could not squander any money left to Amy in the will, her share was put into a trust for up to twenty years; however, it was decreed that should Edwin die within that period the funds could then be released to Amy. When Judge Otis died at the age of 84 he put the same wording as his wife in his will, ensuring the money was held in trust so Edwin could not get his hands on it.

Edwin was not at all happy about that arrangement. He made efforts to regain his employment with the Rock Island Line, but was unsuccessful, and further applications to other railroad companies also failed. However, in 1913 he had some luck when he was offered a position with the Great Northern Railroad in St Paul, Minnesota, though at a much lower grade than he had had at the Rock Island Line. The family found themselves on the move again, this time to St Paul, where Amelia was to attend the Central High School. Life was hard for the family, much of the pressure due to the increased household expenses that Amy tried to deal with. Meanwhile, Amelia worked hard at school and demonstrated how bright she was. She was involved in playing a lot of sport, but found herself becoming disillusioned upon observing how boys were favoured above girls – something she found desperately unfair and at odds with her intrinsic belief in equal rights for all. The girls gradually settled down and were finally beginning to enjoy a more social life with their school friends when Edwin told the family that he had been offered another job at the Burlington Railroad's office in Springfield, Missouri, replacing a man who was retiring. Edwin and the family travelled to Springfield in 1914 only to find that the man he was to replace had decided not to retire after all. This was too much for Amy and she made the decision to take the girls to stay with friends in Chicago to give them some stability. The girls attended school and Amelia made every effort to study hard, graduating from Hyde Park High School in 1916.

Meanwhile, Edwin went back to Kansas City and lived with his own family while he established his law practice. He made significant progress in untangling his life, and his efforts impressed Amy enough for her to decide to return to him, with the girls, to live in Kansas City, although it must be said the girls were not very keen on the idea.

Once together again both Edwin and Amy were keen to get their financial situation under control and attempts were made to take control of her inheritance that was in trust. On examination of the trust fund, however, it was discovered that it had been inefficiently managed by her brother, Mark, so Amy took legal action to seize control of it. During this process Mark died and the courts finally ruled that Amy could take charge of all assets.

Amy had been concerned over Amelia and Muriel's education and was now in a position to send them to private schools in preparation for college. Amelia was to attend Ogontz School for Girls in Philadelphia, Pennsylvania, as a boarder, commencing in October 1916, while Muriel went to St Margaret's College in Toronto, Canada.

Amelia found Ogontz a new sort of challenge. Life there involved getting up at 7 a.m. during the week, or, as Amelia wrote in one of her letters to her parents, getting 'up to a cow bell'. It was then to prayers and exercises, breakfast, classes until 2 p.m., then sports and games activities until 4 p.m., at which time they returned to their studies, dinner and further study until bedtime. Other activities during the week included language classes and lectures, but Saturday and Sunday nights were free, although they had to work during the day.

In reference to her studies and sports activities until bedtime, Amelia commented in her letter, 'You see every minute is accounted for and you have to go by schedule.' This was a way of life that rather appealed to Amelia, and she appeared to thrive on it.

While at Ogontz School for Girls, Amelia considered her options for a future career and started to keep a scrapbook of the jobs that women were involved in. She studied the life and work of famous women pioneers in varied professions and from all walks of life to identify how they were able to succeed as 'women working in a man's world'. This was something that was extremely important to Amelia, as she was determined that she would make a success of her life and become a champion for women's rights in the workplace.

In 1917, the United States entered the First World War and Amelia became involved with the Red Cross at Ogontz, taking first-aid courses and knitting clothing for American servicemen. Her independent nature was beginning to show through during her time as a boarder, and she was no longer being moved around from house to house and city to city as a result of her father's job. Furthermore, Amelia was freed from the responsibility of mediation in her parents' marital problems.

Amelia had a quiet nature and was seen at the school to be a 'bit of a loner', most likely due to her strong desire to focus on her learning. Unfortunately, the classes were disrupted by poor behaviour, largely due to the weak teacher being unable to control the class. Amelia decided to try to do something about it, so she organised a petition with two other girls requesting that their teacher should be replaced with a teacher who could maintain control and effectively teach them something. She presented it to the class, but the majority ignored it and subsequently kept away from her, isolationg her further. Amelia was not a loner by nature, she just wanted to get on with her learning, and she couldn't understand why the other girls didn't feel the same way she did. It was an example of peer pressure and bullying at its worst; surely other girls would have signed the petition and supported Amelia, but they were too afraid to stand by their classmate, or even be seen with her after that.

For the summer holiday Amelia spent her time with some close friends at Camp Gray, Lake Michigan, where her interest in young men began to blossom. Amelia returned to Ogontz in the autumn with a fresh outlook on life. Despite the alienation she had suffered as a result of her strong self-discipline and outspoken views (which even saw her get into hot water with the headmistress, who had cause to have serious words with her), her leadership qualities steadily began to be recognised by her peers and by the school management. As a result, Amelia was elected vice president of her class, and was one of five students elected to the board that monitored the school's honour system.

'BEING A MECHANICAL PERSON'

In her book *The Fun of It* Amelia commented on aspects from her childhood experiences that she felt led her into aviation:

Looking back I can see certain threads in what I did that were fully as important in leading me to aviation as being a mechanical person was:

My father being a railroad man and the many trips we had together, by which I discovered the fascination of new people and places.
Liking all kinds of sports and games and not being afraid to try those that some of my elders in those days looked upon as being only for boys.
Liking to experiment and try new things.

There they all are, weaving in and out and here and there through the years before aviation and I got together.

For the Christmas holiday of 1917 Amelia joined her sister in Toronto because neither Amelia nor Muriel could afford to go all the way to California, where their parents lived at the time. It was in Toronto that Amelia came into contact for the first time with the effects that the First World War had on the Canadian troops who had returned from the fighting in France. In her book *20 Hrs., 40 Min.* Amelia wrote, 'Four men on crutches walking together in King Street in Toronto that winter, was a sight which changed the course of existence for me.' She decided that after her Christmas break she would stay and help in the hospitals. She wrote to her parents to tell them that she was not returning to Ogontz, but her mother warned her that it would mean giving up on graduating. However, Amelia had already decided that it was impossible for her to return to Ogontz; she was desperate to help the wounded Canadian

Amelia as a nurse. (Courtesy of Mary S. Lovell)

troops. She wrote to her headmistress to tell her that she would not be returning, then started her training under the Canadian Red Cross and became a nurse's aide at the Spadina military hospital.

While at the hospital, Amelia worked from 7 a.m. to 7 p.m., with just two hours off in the afternoon. Although the nurse's aides assisted in the wards by scrubbing floors and undertaking tasks that gave the sisters and nurses more time to deal with patients, they would also play tennis or 'walk and talk' with the recovering men. In *20 Hrs., 40 Min.*, Amelia describes the patients calling her 'sister' and having to rush around dealing with their many requests. There were times when a patient would ask Amelia, 'Please rub my back, sister' (remembering some of the 'lovely backs' she said she had rubbed!). However, Amelia recalled that more of her time was spent at first in the diet kitchen and later in the dispensary, due to her knowledge of chemistry, and with a touch of humour added, 'Probably the fact that I could be trusted not to drink up the medical supply of whisky counted more than chemistry.'

During what leisure time she had Amelia would visit some of men she had looked after in the military hospital at Amour Height's military airfield near Toronto. While there she saw pilots in biplanes practising take-offs and landings and talked over matters relating to flying with them. Most of them had learned to fly during the First World War but following the Armistice there was very little work around, so some tried to make a living by barnstorming around the United States and Canada. They demonstrated their aerobatic skills and also gave flights to an increasingly interested public. Amelia's visits further stimulated her interest in aviation, but they were to be cut short by a period of serious illness.

Automobile mechanics course at college. Amelia is third from the right. (Courtesy of Mary S. Lovell)

Troops returning from the battlefields brought with them a deadly form of influenza. Amelia, who was working long days, was also one of the few nurse's aides asked to work nights. She would go around with a bucket of medicine and ladle it out to the patients. Unfortunately, she caught influenza and developed a serious pneumococcal infection – a very painful infection in her sinus, known today as sinusitis. After an operation to drain and repair the cavity came a long period of convalescence, and she was still recovering when the war ended on 11 November 1918. This was the day when excited young men ran around throwing flour over women as they celebrated.

In the spring of 1919, while convalescing, Amelia visited Northampton, Massachusetts, to join her sister, who was studying to prepare for entry to Smith College. Amelia was musically talented, and while at Northampton she learned to play the banjo and also joined an all-female class to learn how to repair car engines. This, she later said, 'laid the foundation of any practical knowledge of motors I have gained since'. Their mother, Amy, joined them at Northampton and was keen to spend time with her daughters. Amy felt more comfortable with her finances, due to being able to use the money from the trust fund, and decided to take the girls to Lake George in New York State for the summer. This was a restful time for Amelia and was just what she needed while she recovered from her illness. While on holiday she started to think about what to do next. After her experience as a voluntary nurse, she felt that she would like to study to be a doctor and so she enrolled at Columbia University.

Muriel was to study at Smith College while Amelia left Northampton to begin her medical studies at Columbia University in New York. During her time there, Amelia started to undertake some more daring escapades. She discovered how to get the key to the roof of the university library and would climb up the many steps to the roof and then over the top of the dome to spend time gazing into the night sky. At this time, she was beginning to demonstrate her support for the struggle for women's rights to vote and her conviction that girls and women should have the same chances as men. Nevertheless, it appears that, once at Columbia, Amelia began to question whether she had the necessary skills to become a medical practitioner and she was eventually to drop out in 1920.

In the meantime, her father, who had by then overcome his alcoholism, had decided to move from Kansas City to Los Angeles, with a view to increasing opportunities for his law practice, and wanted to have his family with him. Amy, while not happy to return to her husband, wanted her girls to go with her. Muriel did not want to leave Smith

College, so Amelia's parents wrote to her informing her that her father had found a job there and requested that she join them in California. Amelia, a loyal daughter, did as she was asked. It is possible that Amelia's decision to leave Columbia may have been partially formed by pressure from her mother to go with her to help repair what was an unhappy marriage. Indeed, Amelia had already told Muriel that she intended to return to the east as soon as it was possible to get her own life back. In *The Fun of It* she wrote, 'But when you are young, you are apt to make important decisions for reasons that later become quite superficial. And I decided against medicine in just this way, hearkening to the pleadings of my mother and father, leaving Columbia and going to California.'

LEARNING TO FLY AND EARLY SUCCESSES

Once in California, Amelia began to adjust to a lifestyle that she liked: the climate was good and she felt comfortable in the family home. There was no end of open-air activities for her to try and she discovered there was a huge interest in flying out west. Amelia, who was already keenly interested in aviation, enjoyed being able to go to the large number of flying displays with her father. By that time, aircraft were never far from her thoughts and she was inspired by what she saw at such events. One Sunday, Amelia went to an air meet at Long Beach with her father and saw a pilot in a flying suit. She asked Edwin to find out how long it took to learn to fly and how much the lessons cost. Her father spoke to the pilot and was told that it could take between five and ten hours, depending

JN-4 Canuck. (Courtesy of 1000aircraftpictures.com, Jim Brink and Ed Garber Collection)

on the ability of the learner. The price of the lessons came as a shock to Edwin when he was advised they would cost up to $1,000, a figure he could ill afford. However, Edwin wanted to give his daughter a treat and paid $10 for her to have a ten-minute flight with Frank Hawks, an ex-army pilot who would go on to make his name as a 'speed king'. Amelia was put in the front cockpit and as soon they had taken off she knew she had to fly. However, she was not impressed with Hawks' negative attitude towards potential female pilots and decided she would feel more confident with a female instructor.

Amelia went home and told her family she wanted to learn to fly. Her father thought it might be possible and gave his support to the idea. He was perhaps hoping Amelia would change her mind, but he took her to Kinner Field, Los Angeles, to meet Neta Snook, the only woman instructor in southern California, and to find out how much she charged for lessons.

Snook had learned to fly in 1917, just before the USA entered the First World War, and was the first woman to graduate from the Curtiss School of Aviation. She bought and restored a Canuck, which was a Canadian version of the American Curtiss JN-4, and then went barnstorming around the United States. Snook became a flying instructor after negotiating with Bert Kinner for permission to use his new airfield to set up her company.

When Neta first met Amelia she was taken by how elegant she looked, while she was dressed in dirty, greasy overalls. She was impressed by Amelia and took a liking to her immediately. Amelia explained she wanted to learn to fly and asked Neta if she would teach her. However, when her father realised how expensive the lessons were he said he could not afford that sort of money, so Amelia got a job in the office of a telephone company to help foot the bill. Neta, who had already built up a lot of flying experience, was then aged 24, just one year older than Amelia. She was exactly the instructor Amelia needed, and she even allowed Amelia to have lessons on credit, which helped her on-going financial problems.

Amelia's first lesson took place on 3 January 1921, when Neta took her up in the Canuck, and within a month she had logged four hours' flying time. Neta became quite friendly with Amelia's family and often visited her at home. This was a time when romance was blossoming for both women. Neta had a serious boyfriend and Amelia had become friendly with Sam Chapman, who was lodging at her parents' house with two other young men. Sam was in love with Amelia and said he would eventually like to marry her. Amelia, on the other hand, was not looking for marriage and, as Neta observed, seemed more interested in older men because she felt they were more relaxed and unlikely to expect as much from a girl as a younger man might. While conducting her flying lessons Neta also

Neta Snook with Amelia Earhart on her first training flight, 3 January 1921. (Private collection of Karsten Smedal, Courtesy of Ames Historical Society)

gave Amelia driving lessons in a T-Model Ford, which they had rented.

Amelia had observed Kinner, the owner of the airfield, working on one of his aircraft, which he had named the 'Airster'. She was becoming more interested in buying her own plane and found herself drawn to this particular one. Despite warnings from the other pilots that the Airster lacked power, she decided it was the one she wanted. The price tag was $2,000, and at first her father offered to help her to buy it, but later changed his mind. Amelia gathered all the money she had, and also asked her sister if she could help, although that was not possible as she was still at college. Undaunted, Amelia taught herself photography, but found she could not make money from it until she got a job in a photographic studio. Her mother was not

Amelia with her first plane, a Kinner Airster. In this photograph Amelia is wearing Neta Snook's coat. (Private collection of Karsten Smedal, Courtesy of Ames Historical Society)

Neta Snook and Amelia, 1921. (Courtesy of Mary S. Lovell)

happy that Amelia was working and offered to contribute towards the cost, provided she quit and stayed at home. This she did at first, but it couldn't last and Amelia had to get a job first as a telephone operator and then a second one as a truck driver, to cover her flying costs, as she was keen to fly as much as possible. Once Amelia had bought her new plane she named it the 'Canary' because it had been painted bright yellow.

To maintain and hangar the aircraft was very expensive, but Kinner came to the rescue by offering her free space and help with the maintenance in return for her help in demonstrating the Kinner Airster to potential customers.

Amelia continued with her flying lessons but it was not long before she had her first crash. Neta was her co-pilot when the aircraft stalled, although it was not badly damaged and neither woman was hurt. A second incident happened because no one had checked the fuel levels before take-off, so the aircraft ran out of fuel and crashed, damaging the landing gear and propeller. Amelia could be very conscious of her appearance and after one crash Neta said she saw her powdering her nose before talking to reporters.

Neta believed Amelia was ready to fly solo after logging nine hours' flying time (five hours in the Canuck and four in the Airster), but having had two accidents, Amelia was determined not to rush things. She was keen to learn all she could before flying alone and that included

Amelia's first crash into a cabbage patch in 1921. (Courtesy of Mary S. Lovell)

mastering all the manoeuvres needed for stunt flying. To do this she started to take advance instruction with John Montijo, a First World War flying ace, and after a few weeks of lessons she felt ready to go solo. Her first flight was not without mishap: one of the shock absorbers broke, forcing Amelia to land and have repairs carried out. With some trepidation, she took off again, climbed to 5,000ft and flew around for a while before, in her own words, she 'returned to make a thoroughly rotten landing'.

Amelia began to change her appearance to look more like an aviator. She started by gradually shortening her hair, a small section at a time, so her mother would not notice, and she also bought goggles, a helmet and a leather jacket for $20. To ensure the leather jacket did not look new, she slept in it for a number of nights. Amelia also wore trousers, which she felt comfortable in because they covered her legs and ankles, an area of her body that she had never been happy with. In this attention to her appearance she was in total contrast to Neta, who only ever wore her dusty, creased and oily overalls. As a result, Amelia began to attract the attention of the public, captivated by her stylish, feminine appearance in what was essentially a male-dominated environment.

Amelia's fame as an aviatrix was growing, and on 17 December 1921 she was invited – along with silent-movie star Aloysia McLintic, another aviatrix – to the Pacific Coast Ladies Derby held at the Sierra airfield, East Pasadena, in front of 7,000 spectators. There were twelve different events, including a wide range of stunts and daredevil manoeuvres. Tenth on the programme was Amelia, flying her Kinner Airster, and Aloysia, flying her Laird Swallow; they each carried out a number of intricate stunts to entertain the spectators.

When Amelia's sister, Muriel, came to California for her summer vacation, she too became interested in flying and would turn up at the airfield in riding breeches and boots to watch the planes. In October 1922 Amelia invited her father and sister to a flying display at Rogers Field, California, and they were mystified when she apologised for not being able to sit with them. They soon discovered why when it was announced to the spectators that a young lady was going to try for an altitude record in her own aeroplane. That young lady was Amelia, flying her Kinner 'Canary'. In advance of her attempt on the record, Amelia had asked an official of the Aero Club of Southern California to seal her barograph so that changes could not be made to the recorded altitude. Amelia took off, started to climb and disappeared into the clouds. Despite difficulties with the engine of the Airster above 12,000ft, an hour later she landed to great excitement – she had recorded an altitude of 14,000ft. The aero club official checked the barograph and confirmed that she had broken the women's altitude record. However, the record was not to last long as Ruth Nichols swiftly broke it again. Ruth had learned to fly in 1919 and by 1923 had even flown solo in a seaplane. Her flying credentials were impressive, as she went on to pilot many different types. Ruth would later join Amelia in the formation of an organisation for women pilots called the Ninety-Nines.

Amelia tried for the record again, but this time the weather conditions were not in her favour and once above 10,000ft she ran into thick cloud, followed by sleet and snow at 11,000ft and dense fog at 12,000ft. This was a new experience for Amelia and she decided to put the aircraft into a spin until she ran into clear weather, which she did at about 3,000ft. However, she was approached by an older, more experienced pilot who checked her barograph record and, pointing to the vertical line on the record sheet as a result of her steep descent, asked if she had fallen asleep in the cockpit. When Amelia told him she had initiated the spin in order to dive under the fog, he was not impressed and pointed out, 'What if the fog had lasted all the way to the ground?' That was food for thought for Amelia!

The press became interested in Amelia's activities and the *Los Angeles Examiner* interviewed her for a feature on 8 August 1922. During that interview, Amelia had indicated that she hoped to be able to fly across the continent the following year and suggested she might stop at Vassar College, New York, and enrol on a course. This was the same college that her mother, Amy, had wanted to attend, but her father had not allowed it.

Amelia applied to the Fédération Aéronautique Internationale (FAI) and was awarded flying certificate No. 6017 on 16 May 1923. The FAI had been reorganised as the National Aeronautic Association (NAA), which now allowed women pilots into its membership; Amelia was the sixteenth in the world to be admitted. Amelia received more recognition a month later when she was admitted into the membership of the Aeronautical Hall of Fame, followed by further public acknowledgement of her flying status in the magazine of the Aero Club of America.

Another newspaper article was published in the *New York Times* in October of that year. All of this press intrusion did not go down well with some of Amelia's family, who did not consider such publicity suitable for a 'lady', commenting that the only time a lady's name should appear in the newspaper was in the event of their birth, marriage and death. This attitude did nothing to dissuade

Amelia, who was convinced that gaining publicity was crucial to her establishing a solid reputation as an aviator.

Amelia's mother was now facing more financial hardship after she discovered that only $20,000 of her inheritance remained. The money that had dwindled after paying for the girls' private education shrunk further still after helping Amelia purchase her Airster. Amy needed to look at ways of protecting her capital by finding profitable investment. At that time Amelia was still with Sam Chapman and he had a friend, Peter Barnes, who owned a gypsum mine and wanted to buy two trucks to improve the road links between it and the railroad. With Amelia's encouragement, Amy invested the remainder of her inheritance in the project, but the plan was doomed to be a failure when the mine was flooded and the trucks destroyed. Urgent changes had to be made. Muriel left college to become a high school teacher, while Amelia sold her Airster to a young pilot (who immediately took the plane up with a friend on board to do some stunting and crashed, killing them both). Amelia was devastated at her mother's financial losses after acting on her and Sam's advice, and she received another knock when she became ill with the return of her painful sinus infection.

More problems were brewing for the family in 1924 when her parents' relationship had deteriorated so much that they both agreed to divorce. The decision was made for Amelia and her mother to travel across the country to Boston to join Muriel, who was working there. Amelia had earlier planned to fly from the west coast to the east coast, but she knew that it would have been impossible with her sinus problem. When she sold her plane she had bought a car, a Kissel roadster, which, because of its colour, she had nicknamed 'Yellow Peril'. So instead of flying,

Amelia and her mother drove across the American continent to Boston.

Their trip was extended when Amelia decided to take her mother to visit all the national parks on their journey, which more than doubled the direct-route mileage and took them six weeks to complete. During the trip, Amelia's sinus condition worsened to the extent that, when they arrived at Boston, she had to go to hospital; it took months for her to get back to full health.

Amelia thought about continuing with her studies at Columbia and travelled to New York in the autumn. However, she was still suffering the effects of her illness and decided she needed more time to recover, so she stayed with a friend on Long Island. Eventually, she felt well enough to register and pay for two courses at Columbia, but by now she had very little money left. After just a few months she returned to Boston and later took a course at Harvard. As she was so short of funds she applied for a scholarship at the Massachusetts Institute of Technology, but was unsuccessful. This was another devastating blow to Amelia, now greatly uncertain about what she should do with her future. Muriel was teaching and Amelia thought perhaps that was something she could do herself, so she started taking on part-time teaching jobs in and around the Boston area. She became a member of the Educational Service Bureau of Boston and taught foreign students English as part of the Massachusetts University Extension Department.

Determined to get a permanent post, Amelia eventually applied to Marion Perkins, head worker at Denison House in Boston, for a position as a social worker. She was successful and was appointed as a resident full-time staff worker at $60 a month, commencing in October.

Amelia was to be in charge of the pre-kindergarten and assist the children aged 5 to 14, many of whom were learning English as their second language. Amelia saw her job as a social worker as an opportunity to share with the children the sorts of exciting experiences that she herself had experienced as a young child. It was an ideal job for her and she relished every moment with her charges.

2

THE CHALLENGE OF FLYING THE ATLANTIC

A significant event took place in May 1927 when Charles Lindbergh became the first man to fly solo across the Atlantic in the *Spirit of St Louis*, winning the Orteig Prize of $25,000. The prize was an award given to aviators who flew non-stop from New York to Paris, or vice versa.

At 7.52 a.m. on 20 May, Charles Lindbergh took off from Roosevelt Field, Long Island, for his historic flight to Paris. From New York he headed for Cape Cod and Nova Scotia, and then over the Atlantic, climbing to about 10,000ft, just above the storm clouds. He continued on his course and knew he must be near land when he saw a group of fishing boats. Not quite sure where he was, Charles flew to just a few feet above one of the boats and throttled back, shouting to the fisherman to give him directions for Ireland. That was unsuccessful, so he continued on his course until he came to the Irish coast, and then set his compass course for Paris. He flew over the coast of France and landed at Le Bourget to a huge welcome from the waiting crowd.

Amelia was now working at Denison House and with a steady income she could think about flying again. Bert Kinner still remembered her and suggested to Harold T. Dennison, a Boston businessman, that he should consider having Amelia join him on a project to develop a new airport in the city. Amelia invested some of her own money, becoming a company director, and was at last in a position to be able to afford to fly again. The new Dennison Airport opened in July 1927 and on 3 September Amelia flew on the first official flight out of it. For the next few years she promoted the new airfield in Boston by giving flying lessons and taking part in air displays in the area. Bert allowed her to use his new Airster – a good move for him because it gave her an opportunity to demonstrate the plane to prospective customers.

Amelia was now quite a celebrity as far as the local press was concerned, and she began to use the media more to encourage other women to take up flying. She wrote to Ruth Nichols in the autumn to ask her advice on forming an organisation for women who already flew. It was the first step towards Amelia and Ruth getting together to set up such an organisation.

Amelia gradually realised that her relationship with Sam Chapman was beginning to get in the way of her plans. Sam had moved to a new job in Massachusetts to be near her and was keen for them to get married. However, Amelia had no intention of giving up her new-found independence and broke away from the relationship, although the couple still remained friends. From then on, her life was extremely busy with her work at Denison House and her commitment to more flying after joining the Boston chapter of the NAA. Amelia had always enjoyed writing and poetry and she was inspired to put pen to paper after a meeting at Denison House, at which the women discussed a book entitled *The Challenge of Life*. She focused her thoughts on the way in which her life was developing, went away and wrote the following poem:

> Courage is the price that Life exacts for granting peace,
> The soul that knows it not, knows no release
> From little things;
> Knows not the livid loneliness of fear,
> Nor mountain heights where bitter joy can hear
> The sound of wings.
>
> How can Life grant us boon of living, compensate
> For dull grey ugliness and pregnant hate
> Unless we dare
> The soul's domination? Each time we make a choice, we pay
> With courage to behold restless day,
> And count it fair.

After Charles Lindbergh had completed his solo transatlantic crossing others decided to make the flight as well. They included women aviators among their number but as yet no woman had yet completed the trip, though sadly some of them lost their lives in the attempt.

One of these brave attempts was by Princess Löwenstein-Wertheim (the English-born Lady Anne Savile who married Prince Ludwig of Löwenstein-Wertheim-Freudenberg and so became Princess Löwenstein-Wertheim). Having an interest in aviation well before the First World War, from 1914 the princess had undertaken quite a number of flights as a passenger. After the war she bought a plane and travelled again as a passenger on the Croydon to Edinburgh

Cup Race. She became acquainted with Captain Leslie Hamilton, who was later to recruit ex-bomber pilot Lt Col Frederick Minchin to fly her Fokker F. VIIA monoplane named *Saint Raphael* in the attempt to make an east to west transatlantic crossing in 1927. The aircraft took off from Upavon, Wiltshire, on 31 August 1927, with Princess Löwenstein-Wertheim on board and piloted by Minchin and Hamilton. The plane was later seen flying over the Irish coast before turning towards the open sea. An American tanker, *Josiah Macy*, saw the aircraft later that evening, but that was to be the last sighting and no trace of it or anyone on board was ever found.

Ruth Elder was 21 years old when she learned to fly, and two years later she heard of Charles Lindbergh's flight from New York to Paris. Despite being an inexperienced pilot, she wanted to attempt the transatlantic flight along with her instructor, Captain George Haldeman, as co-pilot and navigator. Although she certainly did do some flying, it is quite probable that her instructor, with his extra experience, would have taken over as the pilot for much of the journey.

They set off from Roosevelt Field, Long Island, on 11 October 1927, flying a yellow Stinson Detroiter named *American Girl* to fly their planned west to east route, which was to fly along the shipping routes for safety despite the distance being longer. They encountered severe stormy weather and were out of contact for some time, causing concern among those waiting to hear from them. Finally a message came through that they were safe after being rescued by a Dutch tanker, which took them to the Azores. On the flight, the aircraft had developed a serious oil leak and had caught fire just as it was being lifted on to the ship, completely destroying the airframe. Although

Ruth did not succeed in crossing the Atlantic, her fame spread nonetheless and she had a brief Hollywood career as an actress in silent films.

Another attempt at a transatlantic crossing took place in the same month when a Junkers seaplane, registration number D-1230, left Amsterdam for Lisbon carrying a crew of four, with Lilly Dillenz, a Viennese actress, as a passenger. Their planned route was to cross the Atlantic from Lisbon to the Azores and then on to Newfoundland, completing their flight at New York. While in the Azores Lilly met Ruth Elder, who had just arrived on the rescue ship after coming down in the Atlantic. When Lilly later attempted to take off for the flight to Harbour Grace, Newfoundland, it was discovered that the propeller was bent, forcing the cancellation of the crossing.

A fourth attempt was made by Frances Wilson Grayson, a niece of President Woodrow Wilson. She bought a Sikorsky S-36 amphibian plane that she named *Dawn*. The crew for the flight included pilot Oskar Omdal, navigator Brice Goldsborough and radio operator Frank Koehler. They took off from Curtiss Field, Long Island, on 23 December 1927 bound for Harbour Grace in Newfoundland. Later, a radio message was received from them saying something was wrong and after that there was no more communication. It was finally concluded that they must have encountered a fierce storm that caused them to go down into the sea.

Elsie Mackay was a British actress with the stage name Poppy Wyndham and was the daughter of Lord Inchcape. She had learned to fly in 1923 and harboured the ambition to be the first woman to cross the Atlantic. Impressed by the aircraft that Ruth Elder had used in her 1927 attempt, she bought a similar Stinson Detroiter and named it *Endeavour*. In strict secrecy, Elsie and Walter Hinchcliffe took off from RAF Cranwell on 13 March 1928 for their attempt at an east–west Atlantic crossing. The aircraft was seen by a lighthouse keeper at Mizen Head, Cork, Ireland, and later by a French steamer, but this was the last sighting. It was believed to have gone down in the sea when a wheel from the aircraft's undercarriage, with a serial number on, was washed ashore at Donegal in north-west Ireland in December 1928.

Even after the loss of three of the five women who had so far tried to cross the Atlantic there were still others who were planning to make the attempt, and just one month after Elsie Mackay disappeared Amelia was approached to see if she would be interested in taking part in an important flight that could well prove to be hazardous.

FLYING THE ATLANTIC FOR THE FIRST TIME

Amelia found writing for magazines began to take up much of her time and she was always willing to be interviewed if it meant she could promote women aviators. However, in April 1928 her life took a new turn when she was called to the telephone while working at Denison House. She had been busily sorting children into their various groups for after-school activities and initially told the messenger that she was too busy and to tell whoever it was that they should call back later, unless the call was more important than her work. She was told that the call was important and, when she finally took the receiver, she spoke to a gentleman who introduced himself as Captain Railey and asked her if she would like to take part in a flight that had the potential to be full of danger. Amelia was a little shocked, but interested in what he had to say. As she did not know him, she asked for his personal references. After he sent these Amelia agreed to meet him in his office, where he asked her if she would like to be the first woman to fly across the Atlantic. Amelia was intrigued and gave a short rundown of her flying experience of 500 hours and told him she had achieved the women's altitude record of 14,000ft in 1922. As Mary S. Lovell wrote in her book *The Sound of Wings*, Railey was 'struck by the strong resemblance to Lindbergh and immediately coined the sobriquet "Lady Lindy" in his mind'.

Railey, who had been involved in Admiral Byrd's Antarctic expedition, was initially informed that another woman had planned to make a transatlantic flight, but for personal family reasons could no longer do so. This woman still wanted the flight to happen and it was important to her that an American woman should be the first to cross the Atlantic by air. That person was Mrs Frederick Guest of London, formerly Amy Phipps of Pittsburgh. She had acquired a Fokker F.VIIb/3m tri-motor aircraft from Admiral Byrd and had named it *Friendship* as a symbol of goodwill between her own and her adopted country.

Railey had been contacted by George Palmer Putnam, the New York publisher, to assist him in finding a suitable

Byrd Fokker tri-motor. (Courtesy of 1000aircraftpictures. com, David Horn Collection)

replacement who would be willing to take part in the flight. After asking various friends, one of whom was a member of the Boston chapter of the NAA, he was told that there was an enthusiastic young aviator who worked as a social worker, and that she was possibly the person he was looking for.

Amelia did not know at first whether it would be ultimately decided that she was the right person for the job, or whether the flight would even take place, and so endured a period of waiting. At the time, the staff at Denison House were working out their plans for the summer school and Amelia was heavily involved in that work. She was preoccupied about what might happen, but could not say anything to anyone as she was sworn to secrecy over the possible Atlantic attempt.

After about ten days Amelia was invited to New York to meet David T. Layman, Jr, and John S. Phipps, the brother of Amy Guest, and they gave her more information about the project. She would be crossing the Atlantic as a passenger, with Wilmer Stultz as the pilot and Louis Gordon as the flight engineer. Although both pilot and mechanic would be paid for the flight, there would not be any payment for Amelia, but she nonetheless saw this as an ideal opportunity for furthering her aviation career. Amelia understood that they were weighing her up and realised the importance of the meeting. George Putnam, also present, was impressed and decided that Amelia should be chosen. A few days after the meeting, Amelia was contacted and told the flight was going to take place and that she was invited to go along. Despite Amelia's certain knowledge of the fatalities that had occurred during other attempts to make the Atlantic crossing, and the potential dangers she might encounter, there was only one answer – Yes!

Publicity photograph taken in a Boston hotel before the first transatlantic flight in 1928. (Courtesy of Mary S. Lovell)

The whole project was to be kept secret, as was the purchase of the Fokker, because Mrs Guest wanted to avoid attracting any attention. As part of the ruse, preparations to equip the plane were attributed to Admiral Byrd's forthcoming Antarctic trip, and it was claimed that Wilmer 'Bill' Stultz and Louis 'Slim' Gordon had been employed by Byrd to fly the plane with Commander Robert Elmer, of the US Navy, in charge of the technical work. Floats were fitted to the plane in case it had to land on water.

Meanwhile Amelia, who had been relatively active in the Boston chapter of the NAA, had been elected its first woman vice president, and was quite settled with the balance between her flying activities and work as a social worker. She seemed to look upon the trip as an exciting venture, but fully intended to return to her work at Denison House after the journey was over. While waiting to hear when the crossing would commence, Amelia still had to keep the plans secret from the other staff, with the exception of manager Marion Perkins, who needed to know so that she could arrange for a replacement while she was away. Perkins wrote in the foreword of *20 Hrs., 40 Min.*, 'The day she told me of the trans-Atlantic project, and swore me to secrecy, she said, "And I'll be back for summer school. I have weighed the values and I want to stay in social work".'

Amelia kept well away from any of the work being conducted on the *Friendship* and only saw the plane twice before the actual flight. She did not take part in any of the test flights with Bill and Slim and it was not until the first time the plane took off from water that she became actively involved. As the whole intention was for a woman to be the first to fly across the Atlantic by air it was made official that Bill was the pilot and Slim the flight engineer, with Amelia Earhart named the commander.

All the tests, including the radio, were now conducted, with Amelia commenting, 'With the radio we were particularly fortunate because the Stultz is a skilful operator.' The plane was ready to go but the ominous weather reports, being effectively dealt with by Dr James H. Kimball of the US Weather Bureau, did not permit them to depart. For quite a time the weather remained unfavourable, preventing any attempts to take off. Putnam had hoped that the flight would take place on 20 May, the anniversary of Lindbergh's flight the year before, but with the adverse weather reports coming in it appeared very unlikely that date would be achieved.

The crew had waited at Boston for almost three weeks, which they found particularly frustrating because, while the weather was unfavourable in the mid-Atlantic, it was fine in Boston. The team spent some of their time sightseeing in Amelia's old Kissel roadster or sheltering in restaurants or theatres on the rainy days.

When the weather finally improved, the *Friendship* made two attempts to take off but had to land back on the water because initially there was too much fog and then not enough wind. This was a disappointment to the waiting press and camera crews as they were keen to be present when the plane made a successful take-off, but the secrecy was such that when they took off for the third time, successfully, very few observers were present.

It was not until 2 June that the weather forecast for both the take-off and the conditions over the Atlantic were favourable enough for them to set off. Amelia wrote in *20 Hrs., 40 Min.*, 'Three thirty! Another day. Another start. Would it flatten out into failure like its predecessors?'

She described how the whole party 'trooped' out of the hotel before dawn and drove to T Wharf to board the tugboat *Sadie Rose*. The plane at the time was moored off the Jeffrey Yacht Club in East Boston. Amelia, the pilot and the engineer climbed on board, started the engines and taxied down the harbour. They then took off, flying north-east for Newfoundland, as recorded in Amelia's log book, 'We are flying at about 2000 feet. There is a slight haze and the ocean is smooth, with a little colour. From a height it looks quiet, almost like ice with flecks in it.'

It was just after take-off that they had their first emergency: the spring lock of the cabin door broke off. Amelia wrote in her log, 'I had to hold the door shut until Slim could get back to repair it. It was first anchored to a gasoline can, but I saw the can being slowly pulled out, so anchored myself to it instead.'

When they arrived over Halifax, Nova Scotia, they ran into thick fog and had to land. An hour later they took off again to try to make Trepassey, a fishing village on the southern shore of Newfoundland, but the foggy conditions were so bad that they had to return to Halifax and spend the night there. The next morning they took off early for Trepassey and then flew at 2,000ft, with a clear view of the land and sea below. Amelia was feeling the cold, a result of the altitude at which they were flying, but they landed at Trepassey to a very warm welcome from the local people, who had come out in small boats and circled the plane. Amelia was hailed as the first woman to come to Newfoundland, but she was puzzled – did they mean the first woman to fly into Trepassey? The precise meaning did not matter; Amelia said she was honoured to be welcomed in such a way.

The actual crossing of the Atlantic was put back repeatedly for ten days due to the stormy weather. Some of their attempts to take off failed, despite the crew having the wind they had been waiting for, because the receding tide created a heavy sea that swamped the engines with spray, causing them to cut out. Further attempts were also unsuccessful. However, their despair lifted for a time when they all took part in a musical evening, and Amelia commented that one bit of news cheered them up as well: the successful flight of the *Southern Cross* from San Francisco across the Pacific. This was another Fokker tri-motor powered by Wright Whirlwind engines, a type very similar to the *Friendship* but not equipped with floats. Amelia wrote, 'They made it; so could we. Their accomplishment was a challenge.'

In the intervening time before their final successful take-off there was a lot of waiting around, as well as increasing concern over Bill's drinking. Slim warned that if it continued like this Bill might not be sober enough to fly and urged that a replacement pilot be employed to take over. Despite this request, Amelia, with the experience of her own father's alcohol problems behind her, encouraged Bill to take walks with them along the beach. As commander of the flight she saw it as her responsibility to prevent any messages of concern getting back to the sponsors, and it was her decision as to whether it was safe enough to go ahead with the flight.

Finally, on 17 June, a message came from Dr Kimball at the Weather Bureau that the weather for the next forty-eight hours over the North Atlantic was good enough for an attempt. They immediately got ready to take off and Amelia arranged for a telegraph message to be sent to George Putnam half an hour after they had left. It contained the code word 'Violet', informing him that they were on their way. Due to heavy seas, it took them three attempts to take off, and to do so they still had to reduce the aircraft's weight by leaving behind all the spare fuel cans on board. Amelia, in her bid to keep the flight secret, had still not even told her mother or her sister; the first they knew of it was when they read about it in the newspapers.

In her first log-book entry an hour after leaving, Amelia wrote, 'We have 1500 ft, and both boys are in the cockpit. Me, I am holding down a pile of flying suits, as we left every ounce we could spare at Trepassey and the three cushions were among the things discarded.'

The log books kept a detailed account of the flight: despite the drop in temperature, due to the height, Amelia commented, 'I am not cold, as I got used to cold in Trepassey.' She described the changing weather conditions as they progressed and the food they carried, which included three oranges, malted milk tablets, chocolate, sandwiches and a thermos of coffee. Amelia wrote, 'Somehow I wasn't hungry and, curiously, at the end of the trip there still wasn't any particular desire for food.'

At 4.15 they were at 3,800ft and still climbing when radio contact was made with the British ship *Rexmore*, which said it would contact New York on their position.

Further log-book entries refer to when Bill received their position, which showed they had covered 1,096 miles by 10.30 London time. Amelia commented on the view:

One of the greatest sights is the sun splashing to oblivion behind the fog but showing pink as the last glow of the sky. I wish the sun would linger longer. We shall soon be grey-sheafed. We are sinking in the fog.

4000ft. The light of the exhausts is beginning to show as pink as the last glow of the sky. Endless foggies. The view is too vast and lovely for words. I think I am happy – sad admission of scant intellectual equipment. I am getting housemaid's knee kneeling here gulping beauty.

Amelia was kneeling at the chart table, which was in the front on the port side. From there she took photographs of the view:

On the starboard side of the plane was another window. The table itself, a folding device, was Bill's chart table where he made his calculations. Even though one could stand up in the cabin, the height of the table was such that to see out of the window one had to lean on the table or kneel beside it. There was nothing to sit on, as sitting equipment had been jettisoned to save weight.

A further entry in the log book recorded, 'Bill sits up alone. Every muscle and nerve alert. Many hours to go.' At 3.15 a.m. Amelia could see dawn but still a sea of fog.

Slim and Amelia changed places for a while and extracts from the log book recorded that they were at 10,000ft when thirteen hours fifteen minutes out. They started to descend gradually and it was becoming lighter and lighter. At about 3,000ft, the port engine started coughing a bit. The radio had ceased to work so there was no opportunity to make contact with any ocean liners below. Amelia wrote:

Can't use radio at all. Coming down now in a rather clear spot. 2400ft. Everything sliding forward.
8.50. 2 Boats!!!!
Trans steamer.
Try to get bearing. Radio wont. One hr's gas. Mess. All craft cutting our course. Why?

Friendship flying over SS *America*. (Courtesy of Mary S. Lovell)

They returned to their original course after circling the steamer, which, although they did not recognise it at the time, was the SS *America*. Amelia took a photograph, apparently the first one taken of a vessel at sea from a plane in transatlantic flight. They were flying at 500ft due to poor visibility when they saw a fishing boat and then what seemed to be a fleet of fishing vessels. The fuel was running low, with just one hour left, but they knew they must be nearing land, and any land would do! Amelia logged, 'Soon several islands came into view, and then the coastline. From it we could not determine our position, the visibility was so poor. For some time we cruised along the edge of what we thought was typical English countryside.'

Owing to the shortage of fuel, Bill decided to land. Amelia wrote, 'After circling a factory town he picked out the likeliest stretch and brought the *Friendship* down on it. The only thing to tie to was a buoy some distance away and to it we taxied.'

They could see three workmen working on a railway track. They waved at them and Slim shouted, but all they did was walk down to the shore and look over at the *Friendship*, and then they returned to their work.

Amelia standing in the doorway of *Friendship* at Burry Port. (Courtesy of Mary S. Lovell)

People started to gather on the shoreline. Amelia recalled, 'I waved a towel desperately out the front windows and one friendly soul pulled off his coat and waved back.'

It took almost an hour before boats came out to see them and they found out they had landed at Burry Port, South Wales. Bill went ashore and telephoned their friends in Southampton. This alerted Captain Railey, who arrived in a seaplane with Captain Bailey of Imperial Airways and Allen Raymond of the *New York Times*. Amelia, who was seated in the doorway of the *Friendship*, saw Railey on the shoreline. He shouted over his congratulations to her, asking her how it felt to be the first woman to fly the Atlantic. Amelia replied that it was a good experience, adding, 'I was just baggage, just like a sack of potatoes.' She added that she hoped in the future she may be able to make the flight across the Atlantic on her own.

It soon became clear to Amelia that, because she was the first woman to make the crossing, she was the one the reporters wanted to question. She later wrote, 'I tried to make them realise that all the credit belonged to the boys, who did all the work. But from the beginning it was evident the accident of sex – the fact that I happened to be the first woman to have made the Atlantic flight – made me the chief performer in our particular sideshow.'

Due to their tiredness and urgent need for rest, the decision was made to stay overnight in the Ashburnham Hotel and then fly to Southampton the next day. They took off from Burry Port the next morning and Amelia was able to pilot the plane for a while, but Bill took over for the landing on Southampton Water, guided by the green lights of a signal gun showing them where to land. They arrived to a warm welcome from the official launch. On board was Mrs Guest, owner of the *Friendship*, her son and Hubert Scott-Paine, director of Imperial Airways. When they arrived on shore they were welcomed by Mrs Foster Welch, Mayor of Southampton. After the official greetings, the crew went to the South Western Hotel, where many ocean liner passengers stayed before their transatlantic voyages. Once there they were questioned

Amelia, Bill and Slim being welcomed by a large crowd on arrival at Southampton Docks on Tuesday 19 June 1928. (Courtesy of Mary S. Lovell)

Friendship in Southampton Docks. (Courtesy of Mary S. Lovell)

by the press, but yet again all the attention was on Amelia, despite her attempts to praise the work of the crew who actually flew the plane.

Amelia then travelled in Scott-Paine's Rolls-Royce to London, where she was to stay with Mrs Guest in Park Lane. On the way they passed Winchester Cathedral and Amelia, realising it may be the only chance she would get to see it, asked to stop for a short time so she could go in and have a look around. Eventually they arrived at Park Lane and were greeted by Mrs Guest. As Amelia had arrived with no clothes except the ones she was wearing, Mrs Guest took her to Selfridges to buy a wardrobe for all the special functions she was to attend. These included a party at the American Embassy, dancing with HRH, the Prince of Wales, and meeting a number of VIPs, including Winston Churchill, Lady Astor and Lady Mary Heath.

Amelia also received a message of congratulations from President Calvin Coolidge from the White House, dated 18 June, which stated:

> I wish to express to you, the first woman successfully to fly the North Atlantic by air, the great admiration of myself and the people of the United States for your splendid flight. Our pride in this accomplishment of our country-woman is equaled only by the joy over her safe arrival. The courageous collaboration of the copilot, Mr. Wilmer Stultz, and Mr. Gordon, likewise merit our cordial congratulations.
>
> Calvin Coolidge

One morning while still in England, Amelia went by taxi to Croydon Airport, where she had permission to go up in Lady Mary Heath's Avro Avian biplane. As Amelia

Flight with British pilot Captain White. (Courtesy of Mary S. Lovell)

had no licence to fly over British soil she had to take an English pilot up with her. Lady Heath had flown the plane solo from Cape Town to London and agreed to sell the plane to Amelia. Amelia only had a little money of her own and it is thought George Putnam advanced the funds, being fully aware that Amelia was now in a prime position to earn large sums of money from appearances, lectures and sponsorship.

On 28 June, Amelia, Bill and Slim boarded the United States Line vessel SS *President Roosevelt* under the command of Captain Harry Manning, who was later to be a navigator on Amelia's subsequent flights. When the SS *President Roosevelt* arrived in New York the three aviators were welcomed by the mayor and treated to a ticker tape parade, followed by more parades in Boston and

Bill, Amelia and Slim on their welcome home after the first transatlantic flight made by a woman in 1928. (Courtesy of Mary S. Lovell)

Chicago. From this one adventure, despite not having flown the aircraft herself, Amelia had stepped into the role of a celebrity and from then on her life was to change immeasurably. George Putnam came to the forefront, using his experience in representing high-profile individuals and organising their book launches. He immediately arranged for Amelia to stay at his house in Rye, New York, where she would have the space and time she needed to write her story, a story he planned to publish as soon as possible to capitalise on her new-found celebrity status. The book would be titled *20 Hrs., 40 Min: Our Flight in the Friendship.*

Amelia fully intended to return to Denison House to continue the work she loved, and had planned to only make occasional flights from Dennison Airport to maintain her interest in flying. However, she had not realised

Amelia visits the children at Denison House in her Kissel automobile, the Yellow Peril. (Courtesy of Mary S. Lovell)

A group photograph taken on the steps of Langley Research Building. Front row, left to right: E.A. Meyers, Elton Miller, Amelia Earhart, Henry Reid and Lt Col Jacob W.S. Wuest, base commander. Back row, left to right: Carlton Kemper, Raymond Sharp, Thomas Carroll, unknown person behind Amelia and Fred Weick. During her tour of Langley in November 1928, Amelia had part of her raccoon fur coat sucked into the high-speed wind tunnel. (National Archives)

the extent of public interest the Atlantic flight would arouse and it soon looked as if her new status would make it difficult for her return to her old life.

While staying at George's house in Rye, Amelia immersed herself in her writing and spent time with his wife, Dorothy, swimming and shopping. She even took Dorothy up in her Avian after it was shipped over from the UK. Gradually some tension began building between George and his wife over the amount of time he spent working and taking part in other activities with Amelia.

A crash in Amelia's Avro Avian G-EBUG. (Courtesy of Mary S. Lovell)

Their marriage was not secure and George was aware that Dorothy had already had some love affairs, one in particular with a much younger man, but despite this she was still unhappy about the amount of attention her husband was lavishing on the young aviatrix.

When Amelia returned to America in July she quickly realised how inexperienced she was at being a public figure, and she knew she was still not an experienced flyer. Consequently, for the next four years she put her head down and worked hard to gain both types of experience. Despite her determination, she often found the demands of public appearances difficult. She had a love of life but also a strong need for solitude at times, and her burgeoning flying career saw her involved in a number of flying incidents. Progress was not going to be easy.

The Avian that Amelia had bought from Lady Mary Heath had been crated and shipped to the USA from Liverpool on the White Star liner *Baltic*. When it arrived at New York it was reassembled at Curtiss Field and Amelia flew it to Rye. The original UK marking was G-EBUG and when it arrived in America it was given the unlicensed identification mark 7083, with both markings displayed on the aircraft.

Amelia was keen to take the plane up for a test flight and she started to give demonstration flights before deciding it was the time to achieve her ambition to fly across the country from the east to the west coast. Amelia had recently been appointed aviation editor for *Cosmopolitan* magazine and saw this flight as an ideal opportunity to use her experiences of the flight as articles for the magazine.

Amelia left on 31 August with George as passenger, landing at Bellefonte Field for lunch and then heading on to Pittsburgh, but when she attempted to land at Rodgers Field, Pittsburgh, the plane did a ground loop and dropped into an unmarked ditch. It turned up on its nose, seriously damaging the landing gear, propeller and left wing.

George immediately set to work arranging to get the parts needed to repair the plane, but parts for a British type were not easy to acquire. He had to buy a new Avian to get the parts and arranged for a pilot to fly it from Curtiss Field to Rodgers Field, where mechanics got to work to fix the original.

After the Avian was ready, Amelia took off alone and continued her flight solo across the continent, keeping George and her family informed of her progress at each of her stops. The media had by now got hold of the story and were keeping their attention on the flight. It was not smooth sailing for Amelia, as she had to make two forced landings through engine trouble, but fortunately she was not injured.

Navigation was not easy; this was her first long-distance challenge and she had to use outdated maps. Navigating with an open cockpit was difficult, with the maps being blown about and some of them even blowing away. Amelia arrived safely at Los Angeles on 14 September while the National Air Races were on, but she had no intention of taking part this time.

On 30 September Amelia was on her return flight back to New York when she started to have engine trouble and had to make a forced landing in a ploughed field near Tintic, Utah. The Avian tipped up on its nose, causing damage to the propeller. After spending the night at Eureka, Utah, Amelia arranged for the plane to be taken to Salt Lake City for repairs. It was not until 9 October that she could take off again and she finally reached New York on 16 October, returning to the lecture tours to promote her book *20 Hrs., 40 Min*. Amelia had become the first woman to fly across the North American continent and back.

3

RACING AND AUTOGIRO ESCAPADES

Amelia was kept very busy with the many requests and engagements that were booked for her, as well as with writing articles for *Cosmopolitan*. In July 1929 she became assistant to the general traffic manager of Transcontinental Air Transport, the forerunner of Trans World Airlines, joining Charles Lindbergh as consultant, with the the role of encouraging women to travel by air. As a result of her work Amelia was able to travel at times, when she was not inclined to fly herself, on a scheduled airline flight, and she would often take her mother, Amy, to serve as an example to potential women passengers that there was nothing to fear. Amelia maintained regular contact with her family and during the intervening time attended the wedding of her sister and Albert Morrissey, despite a very busy schedule.

Amelia was painfully aware that her acclaim from the *Friendship* flight was fame for travelling 'just as a passenger'. This gave her the incentive to take extra lessons to develop her skills and gain her commercial transport licence, becoming just the fourth woman to do so – the first three being Phoebe Omlie, Ruth Nichols and Lady Mary Heath.

1929 Women's Air Derby. Left to right: Louise Thaden, Bobbi Trout, Parry Willis, Marvel Crosson, Blanche Noyes, Vera Dawn Walker, Amelia Earhart, Marjorie Crawford, Ruth Elder and Florence 'Pancho' Barnes. (Courtesy of Mary S. Lovell)

This achievement, she felt sure, would contribute more to solidifying her reputation as an aviatrix than the celebrity status gained through the *Friendship* flight.

In the spring of 1929 Amelia started to look for a more powerful plane, and after selling her Avian she bought a Lockheed Vega, registration number NC6911 and powered by a 225hp Wright Whirlwind engine, which had been used on the east coast as a demonstration model. It was more than three weeks to the first Women's Transcontinental Air Derby, nicknamed the 'Powder Puff Derby' by Will Rogers, which was to be held as part of the 1929 National Air Races. Amelia wanted to enter that race so she shared the flying of her Vega with army pilot Lt Orville Stephens in order to cross the continent to get to California and prepare for the race. The plane was taken to be checked and tuned up by Lockheed mechanics, but when Wiley Post, a

Lockheed test pilot, flew it he could not believe what a bad state it was in. Lockheed was well aware of Amelia's rising fame and, not wanting any bad publicity, turned the situation to its advantage by exchanging the Vega for a brand new model, registration NC31E.

To enter the Transcontinental Air Derby, pilots had to have 100 hours of solo flying, including twenty-five hours of cross-country flying. Twenty women pilots entered the race, including Florence 'Pancho' Barnes, Ruth Elder, Mary Haizlip, Ruth Nichols, Gladys O'Donnell, Phoebe Omlie, Louise Thaden and 'Bobbi' Trout, who Amelia mentions as 'Twentieth Century Pioneers' in her book *The Fun of It*. The race was to begin at Santa Monica on 18 August and take eight days, ending in Cleveland, Ohio. Fourteen women completed the race, with Louise Thaden winning, Gladys O'Donnell coming second and Amelia finishing

Left to right: Amelia, Ruth Nichols and Louise Thaden. (Courtesy of Mary S. Lovell)

third. However, some competitors were forced to drop out for various reasons, including Florence 'Pancho' Barnes and Ruth Nichols, who crashed their aircraft. Sadly, Marvel Crosson died when her parachute failed to open after her aircraft got into difficulties over Arizona.

Amelia also had some problems during the race. While she had been used to flying lightweight planes it was a different situation with the Vega, which was heavy, not easy to land and one of the fastest in the competition. She had to get used to flying it during the race. While landing at Yuma, Arizona, she ran off the end of the runway and bent the propeller. A new propeller had to be ordered and fitted before she could continue.

On 1 July 1929 Wilmer 'Bill' Stultz, who had been Amelia's pilot on the *Friendship*, was killed when he crashed while stunt flying in a Waco Taperwing at Roosevelt Field, Long Island. He had taken up two young men as passengers who 'wanted some thrills' and started his stunting manoeuvres at quite a low level. However, while in a climb the plane seemed to go out of control and it nosedived to the ground. The crash investigators found two left shoes of different sizes jammed under the rudder bar, making it impossible for the pilot to move it. However, Bill was well known for drinking heavily, as Amelia found out on the *Friendship*, and a few days later the autopsy report revealed that he had been very drunk while flying that day. The two shoes jammed under the rudder bar were thought to be from the two young men, who had hooked their feet under it to stop themselves falling out after becoming terrified by the stunt flying.

The idea of forming an association of women flyers had been broached by Amelia to Ruth Nichols a few years earlier, and after the derby it seemed the right time to get the opinion of the other pilots. Amelia had an informal meeting to gauge their interest, which was followed by a more formal meeting at Curtiss Field on 2 November. Twenty-six women turned up for the talks, which were held in a hangar. There was some disagreement as to what name to give to the group, but Amelia suggested that a letter be sent out to the 117 licensed pilots to see who would be interested in joining an association of women pilots; ninety-nine pilots replied. Consequently, the association became known as the Ninety-Nines and is still running today. At first there was no president, only Louise Thaden as secretary and Blanche Noyes as treasurer. Eventually, Amelia became the first president with Thaden as vice president.

On 22 November, Amelia thought she had broken the women's speed record with a speed of 184.17mph, but it was not recognised by the FAI. Disappointed by this, and supported by George Putnam, she persisted in writing to the FAI and was allowed to make an official attempt on the women's speed record. In June 1930 she set the record at 174.89mph, and on the same day, while carrying 500kg, she achieved 171.43mph. Just ten days later, she set a women's world speed record of 181.18mph over a 3km course.

Amelia continued to travel across the country on her lecture tours and in March 1930 she traded her Vega for a model 5B, registration number NR7952, with a 425hp Pratt & Whitney engine. The plane was painted in a bright red colour and Amelia called it her 'Little Red Bus'. This was the plane that she would use to set a number of important records.

George and Amelia had spent a lot of time together organising events, lecturing and writing, and it became a subject of rumour that their relationship was more than just business, especially when George divorced his wife Dorothy in December 1929. George proposed to Amelia a number of times to no avail – Amelia, with her parents' shaky marriage in her mind, was not interested in getting married. Moreover, she valued her independence too much for that commitment; she had plans for other exciting challenges ahead.

George was protective about Amelia's publicity, even to the extent of threatening the careers of other aviatrix if he thought they were a challenge to her public image. This happened to Elinor Smith, a rising star who had soloed aged 15, set altitude records and solo endurance records and was the youngest pilot to be granted the commercial transport license, among other achievements. To George, however, she was a threat, a potential thorn in the side of his Amelia Earhart publicity machine, and although he said that he would support Elinor in her career, it was a false promise because in the end he made things difficult for her and almost destroyed her career. Nonetheless, Elinor did not give in to the pressure and fought back, doggedly continuing with her flying and undertaking many daring escapades, such as the time she flew under the New York East River bridges, which hit the newspaper headlines because not only did she fly under them but she also had to dodge a US destroyer that was in her flightpath as she passed under the Brooklyn Bridge. In October 1930 Elinor was awarded Best Woman Pilot in America, something George was not at all happy with.

Although Elinor and Amelia were flying colleagues, there was an element of criticism at times from Elinor about the standards of her rival's flying skills, with which she was not impressed. Elinor had been determined to become the first woman to fly solo across the Atlantic and follow in

George Putnam giving Amelia a helping hand climbing into the Beech-Nut autogiro. (Courtesy of Mary S. Lovell)

the footsteps of Charles Lindbergh, but Amelia beat her to it, something Elinor never forgave her for.

Amelia remained very fond of her father, despite his failings, and would visit him as often as possible, especially when he became ill with cancer, which resulted in his death on 23 September 1930. After the loss of her father she seemed to have second thoughts about the idea of marriage. George proposed again while they were in the hangar at the Lockheed factory in Burbank, California, while she was waiting for her plane to warm up. She listened and, with a nod of agreement, she climbed into the cockpit and took off. He was left with the thought that her nod must have been an acceptance and set about arranging their wedding.

Shortly after her father died, Amelia had a serious crash in her new Vega, in Norfolk, Virginia, that caused severe damage to the fuselage. Amelia did suffer some injuries and was lucky they were not too serious, but Lockheed was going to take a considerable time to repair her plane. During this period Amelia became involved with the Pitcairn Company of Willow Grove, Pennsylvania, in the promotion of its new PCA autogiro. In early December Harold Pitcairn invited Amelia to take her first flight with Jim Ray, his chief test pilot.

The autogiro concept was developed by Juan de la Cierva and was the forerunner of the helicopter. The difference was that the autogiro was built in tractor configuration where the engine powers a propeller at the front, as with a plane, with the overhead rotor blades rotating with the flow of air over them and not powered by a motor, as they are on a helicopter. As Amelia wrote in her book *The Fun of It*, 'Like a bird it can settle on the earth and stop – with no roll at all on the ground.' Her first flight was undertaken near Philadelphia when Jim Ray explained what she had to do. Amelia was surprised that it was not to be dual instruction and, after being taken up by Jim for a short flight in which he flew around and then landed, he then got out and said, 'You take her up,' and indicated where he would be standing watching. Amelia remembered the experience in her book: 'Thinking over the moment that the autogiro rose into the air, I am at a loss now to say whether I flew it or it flew me.'

Amelia had been busy with the autogiro flights, but George had not forgotten the nod she gave him when he asked her to marry him and had arranged the wedding for 7 February 1931. The night before the ceremony, Amelia wrote a letter to her future husband stating that she would like it to be an open marriage, and that if did not work out within a year she wanted him to let her go:

Dear GP,

There are some things which should be writ before we are married. Things we have talked over before – most of them.

You must know again my reluctance to marry, my feeling that I shatter thereby chances in work which means so much to me. I feel the move just now as foolish as anything I could do. I know there may be compensations, but have no heart to look ahead.

In our life together I shall not hold you to any medieval code of faithfulness to me, nor shall I consider myself bound to you similarly. If we can be honest I think the difficulties which arise may best be avoided …

Please let us not interfere with the other's work or play, nor let the world see our private joys or disagreements. In this connexion I may have to keep some place where I can go to be myself now and then, for I cannot guarantee to endure at all times the confinements of even an attractive cage.

I must exact a cruel promise, and that is you will let me go in a year if we find no happiness together. I will try to do my best in every way …

AE

George agreed to what she asked and they were married the next day at his grandmother's house in Connecticut.

They did not have a honeymoon as Amelia was busy with her autogiro flights and with planning a transcontinental flight in such a plane from Newark to Oakland. Amelia had become more skilled at flying the autogiro – although she did have a number of accidents in that time – and on 8 April 1931 she set a new altitude record of 18,415ft. At the time there was very little media coverage of her exploits. Amelia had arranged in advance for the NAA to install a sealed barograph before the altitude attempt so that she could have official confirmation of any record she set. Again, Amelia's thoughts were on achieving new firsts and gaining more publicity. She now ordered an autogiro for herself and started to make plans to be the first to fly one across the USA, but she needed sponsorship for the flight. George had accompanied Amelia on her autogiro flights and was looking for a good story so he contacted the Beech-Nut Company for its sponsorship. This was agreed and Beech-Nut took over the order for the autogiro with the proviso that Amelia had the company name in large letters printed on the side.

Amelia had not been well and was looking forward to the transcontinental trip in the autogiro to get back her spirit of adventure. The plan had been to have mechanic

Eddie Gorski aboard to deal with any problems on the east to west coast trip. They left Newark on 29 May and arrived at Oakland on 6 June with the belief that she had become the first autogiro pilot to fly the east–west transcontinental trip. This was not to be the case as another autogiro pilot had just beaten her to the record a week before. Not to be defeated, Amelia immediately set off to aim for the transcontinental record both ways, but as she says in *The Fun of It*, 'I started back from Los Angeles, but alas, did not arrive intact. Texas proved my Waterloo for I had an accident there that considerably damaged the faithful ship.'

That accident had happened when Amelia called in at an air show at Abilene, Texas, to great interest among the spectators, surprised at seeing an autogiro and its woman pilot. After giving some demonstration flights, Amelia was taking off when she was hit by a gust of wind, which brought the autogiro down in among the cars. Although she managed to avoid the spectators, a number of cars were damaged. Neither Amelia nor her mechanic were injured, but the Department of Air Commerce reprimanded her for placing the crowd at risk by poor judgment and control of the autogiro. A replacement autogiro was delivered so she could continue on her eastern route and she eventually arrived back at Newark, New Jersey, on 22 June.

Further autogiro tours continued, but they were not without mishaps. One occurred while taking off from Camden, New Jersey, when the autogiro landed on a fence, and another was at the Michigan State Fairground, Detroit. Amelia was attempting a landing when the autogiro dropped 20ft, completely wrecking the machine. Amelia was not injured, but by this time she was getting

Amelia with New York Mayor James Walker, 1932. (National Archives)

a bit disheartened with flying the autogiro and already had a germ of an idea for her next challenge. She discussed it with George, who was in principle supportive of her plan. Amelia admitted to her husband that she wanted to fly the Atlantic simply because 'she wanted to', and continued:

> It isn't, I think, a reason to be apologised for by man or woman. It is the most honest motive for the majority of mankind's achievements. To want in one's own heart to do a thing for its own sake; to enjoy doing it; to concentrate all one's energies upon it – that is not only the surest guarantee of success; it is also being true to oneself.

The plan was for Amelia to be the first woman to fly the Atlantic solo, following the example of Charles Lindbergh, the first aviator to do so. This challenge had already alerted Ruth Nichols, Elinor Smith and Laura Ingalls, all very experienced and committed aviatrix.

Ruth was experienced in flying many different types of aircraft, and was the only woman to hold simultaneously the women's world speed, altitude and distance records between 1931 and 1932. Elinor was an accomplished flyer from a young age, setting altitude records and solo endurance records. She flew with 'Bobbi' Trout on the first women's refuelling record, as well as being awarded the Best Woman Pilot in America in 1930. Laura Ingalls won the Harmon Trophy in 1934 for the most outstanding female aviator of the year. She was the first woman to fly solo from North America to South America and the first to cross the Andes, in doing so setting a women's distance record of 17,000 miles.

FLYING THE ATLANTIC SOLO

Amelia and George planned in secret for her to fly the Atlantic solo in the Vega. They asked Norwegian Bernt Balchen, an experienced long-distance pilot, and mechanic Eddie Gorski if they could prepare the Vega, which by then had been rebuilt after the crash in Norfolk. They agreed and the plane was then taken to the Fokker plant at Teterboro, New Jersey, where Eddie would work on the modifications under Bernt's direction. These changes would include a new 500hp supercharged Pratt & Whitney Wasp D engine, strengthening of the fuselage, installing new instruments – including a drift indicator, gyroscope and compasses – and the installation of extra fuel tanks to hold 420 gallons, which would be enough to give a range of 3,200 miles. Further plans were made for the use of special Stanavo fuel and oil under the supervision of Major Edwin Aldrin, father of Edwin 'Buzz' Aldrin, the second man to walk on the moon in 1969.

Amelia was immensely satisfied with her choice of Bernt as technical adviser because he was a highly experienced pilot and technician and had experience of going on polar and transatlantic flights with Commander Richard E. Byrd. Her confidence in him was such that it was agreed if Bernt did not think a flight should go ahead, then Amelia would take notice of his advice and pull out.

In order to keep the project secret, George released a cover story to the press that the Vega had been chartered to Bernt, who was at the time working with Lincoln Ellsworth on plans for a flight to the South Pole. George was also working on his plans for the publicity and was hoping the solo flight would take place on 20 May 1932, which would be the fifth anniversary of Charles

Lindbergh's flight. In the meantime, Amelia was working hard day after day on her blind-flying techniques by
practising instrument flying. She also maintained regular
contact with Dr James Kimball in the New York Weather
Bureau for advice on when conditions would be most
suitable to make the flight.

Before Amelia made the transatlantic crossing she
had been completing her book *The Fun of It* and George
said he would hold the last chapter for her to complete
after she had made the flight. In that book, with regard to
Dr Kimball's advice, she wrote:

> On Friday the twentieth, my husband went to town and
> later in the morning I drove to Teterboro to talk things
> over with Bernt and do a little flying. The ship was then
> ready to go. I arrived about 11.30. Eddie Gorski, our
> mechanic at the hangar, told me there was a telephone
> call. It was from my husband, at Dr Kimball's office. They
> had just gone over the morning weather reports, from
> ships at sea, from England and from key stations of the
> United States.

Amelia asked what the weather conditions were like to
Harbour Grace and was told they were 'perfect, fine visibility all the way'. Amelia answered, 'We'll go this afternoon,'
and, deciding there was no time to eat, went home to
change for the trip. After returning to the field, Amelia, Bernt
and Eddie took off twenty minutes later at 3.15 p.m. Amelia
wrote, 'Three hours and thirty minutes later we were at
St John, New Brunswick. Early the next morning we flew to
Harbour Grace in Newfoundland arriving at 2.15pm.'

The plane was made ready for the crossing by Bernt
and Eddie and after a rest Amelia arrived at the aircraft

wearing the only clothes she intended to take, which were jodhpurs, a silk shirt, windbreaker and a leather flying suit. For nourishment she had a thermos bottle of soup, a tin of tomato juice and a straw. Amelia did not want to carry any extra clothes because of her concern about weight. The engine was already running and warmed up, and at 7.12 p.m. she took off and headed into the sunset and out to sea. The weather was fair and Amelia was relaxed and had been flying at 12,000ft for a few hours when the first of her problems arose – altimeter failure. Following this, she ran into a severe storm with lightning and wrote, 'I was considerably buffeted about, and with difficulty held my course.' Eventually Amelia ran into calmer weather and started to climb, but soon realised she was picking up ice as the plane became heavier. As a result she was forced to descend into warmer air, but without her altimeter she was not sure of her height, although she could see breaking waves below her. Amelia recorded:

I carried a barograph, an instrument which records on a disc the course of the plane its rate of ascent and descent, its levels a flight all coordinated with clocked time. My tell-tale disc could tell a tale. At one point it recorded an almost vertical drop of 3,000 feet. It started at that altitude of something over 3,000 feet and ended, well something above the water. That happened when the plane suddenly iced up and went into a spin. How long we spun I do not know. I do know that I tried my best to do exactly what one should do with a spinning plane and regained flying control as a warmth of the lower altitude melted the ice. As we righted, and held level again, through the blackness below I could see the whitecaps too close for comfort.

Foggy conditions made things more difficult and she tried to rise to a level that was below where she was picking up the ice and yet a reasonable height above the waves, tricky to judge without knowing her exact height. By then the journey was completely down to instrument flying and Amelia was very pleased that she had the directional gyro, which she referred to as a 'real life-saver'.

Another problem had arisen about four hours out from Newfoundland when she saw a blue flame appearing through a broken weld on the manifold ring, which she hoped would not get worse.

When daylight arrived she could see the water, but also noticed that some of the ice on the wings had not melted. However, after a short climb she came into sunny conditions. It was now ten hours into the flight and Amelia was keen to keep sight of the water below in case she saw a ship. She did on her approach to the Irish coast, but then spotted what she thought was an oil tanker and decided she needed to look for a place to land. By this time the exhaust manifold was vibrating badly and she found that a fuel leak had started, with fuel dripping from a leaky tank down her neck and shoulders. By this time Amelia knew she would not make Paris and decided to touch down as soon as she found a suitable landing site.

Once over Ireland, Amelia saw a railway track and followed it, knowing it would lead to a town or city that may have an airport. She arrived at Londonderry and circled before deciding on landing in Gallagher's Field at Culmore near Londonderry, which she did at 1.46 p.m. on 21 May. James McGeady and Dan McCallion were mending fences in the field when they saw the red plane come in low and land just a few yards from where they were working. McGeady went up to the plane and watched Amelia climb out, thinking at first she was a man because she was dressed in a shirt and trousers and had short hair. When he asked her if she had come far Amelia replied, 'Only from America.' Amelia had landed on James Gallagher's farm and when he turned up and welcomed her McGeady arranged for her to be given a much needed drink of water. Amelia wanted to telephone

The day after her solo flight in 1932, Amelia is seen reading one of the many telegrams she received to Danny McCallion and the Gallaghers at Culmore near Londonderry. (Courtesy of Mary S. Lovell)

George to say she had arrived safely, but there was no telephone on the farm. Gallagher offered to drive Amelia to the post office in Londonderry, where she was able to telephone George to tell him that she had arrived and had achieved her ambition to be the first woman to fly across the Atlantic. On her return to her plane a great crowd, including the press, had arrived. Amelia stayed for the night at Gallagher's cottage before she was flown by Paramount News to London, where she was met by the American ambassador and stayed the night at the embassy. Amelia was concerned that she did not have anything else to wear, so she asked if she could borrow something. She was then able to visit Selfridges to buy all the outfits she needed for her attendance at the various functions to which she was invited. She also received a message from Lady Astor inviting her to stay.

Amelia was now the first woman to have flown the Atlantic twice, once solo, and was to receive much praise for her achievements, including congratulations from the President of the United States, King George V, the British Prime Minister and Charles and Anne Lindbergh, who sent a cable that read, 'We do congratulate you; your flight is a splendid success.'

Interestingly, the royal family developed an early interest in aviation when King Edward VII, while visiting Paris in 1909, met the Wright Brothers and watched them demonstrate their Flyer. The king had six children: five sons and a daughter. The king's eldest son, Edward, Prince of Wales, served in the Grenadier Guards in the First World War and was given a flight by Maj. William Barker VC in 1918 while he flew the plane with one arm in a sling due to a war injury. When the king found out he immediately banned the young prince from flying, as he was the heir to the throne. His second son, Prince Albert, also served in the First World War in the Royal Navy and then transferred to the RAF in 1919, where he learned to fly and became the first of the royal family to become a qualified pilot. Later, Edward resumed flying and, as Edward VIII, became the first monarch to be a qualified pilot; he also created the King's Flight in 1936. His brother, Prince George, Duke of Kent, earned his pilot's licence in 1930. Amelia had the honour of meeting the Prince of Wales when she was invited to Buckingham Palace, and a few days later danced with him at a charity ball.

George was to sail over on the *Olympic* to Cherbourg, where he met Amelia, who had sailed across the English Channel as a guest of C.R. Fairey in his yacht, *Evadne*. Together, they visited Paris, where Amelia was made a Knight of the Legion of Honour by the French government. They went on to Rome and finally to Belgium, before sailing for New York on the *Ile de France* along with her crated Vega on 15 June. Amelia arrived at New York City early on the morning of 20 June to a rousing welcome, before meeting the Mayor of New York, once again honoured with a ticker tape parade and thousands of people lining the route.

On her return to the United States, President Edgar Hoover presented Amelia with a special gold medal from the National Geographic Society.

Ruth Nichols and Elinor Smith also sent best wishes, a nice gesture that Amelia appreciated, especially as both aviatrix had been planning to fly the Atlantic themselves. The achievement was recognised worldwide and proved beyond all doubt that Amelia was a courageous and capable aviatrix. This was also when Amelia met Louise Thaden for the first time, at Oakland Airport.

Amelia receives the National Geographic Special Gold Medal from US President Herbert Hoover at the White House on 21 June 1932 in honour of her transatlantic flight. In the white suit is Dr Gilbert Grosvenor, president of the National Geographic Society, and on the right is the First Lady, Lou Henry Hoover, watching the presentation. (Courtesy of Mary S. Lovell)

Amelia was fired up to achieve more and already had an idea of her next challenge. She had set her heart on beating the speed record of seven hours thirty-eight minutes set by Frank Hawks on his transcontinental flight. It was only a short time after arriving back in the United States that Amelia and George flew to Los Angeles, where she would take off in her Vega for her attempt on the record. No woman had yet flown non-stop coast to coast and Amelia wanted to be the first to do so.

Amelia took off on 12 July to fly to Newark, New Jersey, but had to land at Columbus, Ohio, due to a clogged fuel line. This wrecked any chance of her making a non-stop solo flight and challenging Hawks's speed record, but she finally arrived in New Jersey in nineteen hours fourteen minutes. The actual flying time was seventeen hours fifty-nine minutes, which set a new women's record for the transcontinental flight by beating Ruth Nichols' previous record time, and it was nearly as fast as Hawks's. Interestingly, it was Hawks who had taken Amelia up for her first flight of ten minutes that her father paid $10 for, and now, just a matter of years later, she was challenging his record.

About this time Amelia became close to Gene Vidal, who was also interested in flying and loved to spend time with aviators. Amelia and Gene had worked together at Transcontinental Air Transport (TAT); they felt a mutual attraction and had a deepening relationship. Gene would visit Rye whether her husband was there or not. George was well aware of the conditions laid down in Amelia's pre-nuptial agreement and went along with it.

The Tenth Olympic Games was being held in Los Angeles, and on 29 July, the day before the games were opened, Amelia was presented with a Distinguished Flying Cross awarded by Congress and presented by Vice President Charles Curtis. Following her presentation, Amelia attended the 1932 Olympic Games, accompanied by George and his son David Binney, and mingled with the sports stars and Hollywood greats while still being acknowledged for her achievements.

After the Games were over, Amelia resumed her flying and on 24 August she took off from Los Angeles to attempt the non-stop solo transcontinental record. She touched down at Newark, New Jersey, after nineteen hours, seven minutes and fifty-six seconds, becoming the first woman to

Amelia organises a flight over Baltimore and Washington for the
First Lady, Eleanor Roosevelt. (Courtesy of Mary S. Lovell)

fly non-stop coast-to-coast. In the process she also broke
Ruth Nichols' distance record. Then it was back to pro-
moting her book through lecture tours and appearances,
and along with her many awards Amelia was awarded the
Harmon Trophy in 1932 for the most outstanding aviatrix,
which she accepted on behalf of 'all women'.

When Franklin Roosevelt was elected US President in
1932, Amelia made frequent visits to the White House,
where she got to know the First Lady, Eleanor Roosevelt.
Amelia discovered that they were very alike, with their
independent natures and competitive and sporting
accomplishments. There were still many things that the
First Lady wanted to do. One wish was to learn to fly,
something for which she needed the president's support,
but it was not forthcoming. However, the First Lady was
to be in for a surprise in the near future.

Amelia and George were invited to the White House as overnight guests in April 1933 and during dinner Amelia asked the First Lady if she had ever experienced night flying. Eleanor said she had not and Amelia, who had already arranged with Eastern Airlines to loan her a Condor aircraft and a crew, took Eleanor Roosevelt, still in evening dress, to the airport. They took off and flew over Washington and Baltimore, giving the First Lady her first experience of a night flight.

4

MORE RECORD-BREAKING FLIGHTS

In June 1933, the organisers of the National Air Races agreed to allow women to compete with men for the first time. Amelia and Ruth Nichols were both keen to enter the Cleveland to Los Angeles Bendix race but knew they could not win, as the men were flying more powerful machines. Very soon into the race Ruth had problems with her plane and took longer to complete the course. Amelia was also having problems with an overheating engine and her hatch cover blew off, so she was surprised to learn that when she landed she received $2,000 for being the first woman to finish. Just a few days later, Amelia took off for a second time to better her transcontinental flight record of 1932, but once more she had problems with the hatch cover; it blew open again and she had to hold it closed for 75 miles until she landed in Amarillo, Texas. There was a further problem when choking fumes in the cockpit caused Amelia to land at Columbus, Ohio, before she finally arrived at Newark, New Jersey, in seventeen hours, seven minutes and thirty seconds, bettering her previous record by almost two hours.

Any accident suffered by women gave the race officials an excuse for excluding them, as was the case when Florence Klingensmith, the first woman to enter the 1933 Frank Phillips Trophy race, crashed and was killed while flying a red Gee Bee Model Y. This tragedy led to officials banning women from further events, including the 1934 Bendix race.

Amelia spent quite a bit of the summer of 1933 resting at Rye, during which time her mother came to visit her. George was on a trip to Europe and generally busy with his full-time work at Paramount Pictures in Hollywood, but the couple did manage to have an extended holiday in the Absaroka Mountains, Wyoming, where they went backpacking. Amelia was already developing plans for her next challenge and told George that she intended to fly 2,405 miles solo from Hawaii to Oakland, California, becoming the first person to do so. George knew this would be a difficult challenge but supported his wife nonetheless and set about raising funds to pay for what was likely to be an expensive flight.

Amelia had made her own clothes for a number of years after she developed an interest in sewing as a child, but her appearance as a young lady was particularly important to her. Later on, when she became a celebrity, many photographs were taken of her, with great attention lavished on what she was wearing. She had become a fashion icon and in the early part of 1934 she started creating her own designs. At first there were ideas for the Ninety-Nines' flying clothes and then came her own design label, Amelia Fashions. Her clothes were manufactured and sold in major department stores in each city, including Macy's in New York. Although the designs sold well the success she enjoyed in this sector was brief. She had a busy schedule of lectures and appearances and the label quickly became too much of a drain on her health, so she

Clothing designs created by Amelia under her label Amelia Fashions.
(Courtesy of Mary S. Lovell)

As well as designing clothes, Amelia promoted her own luggage line, which was marketed as Modernaire Earhart Luggage. (Courtesy of Mary S. Lovell)

closed it at the end of the year. Her other promotions included a luggage line that was marketed as 'Modernaire Earhart Luggage', and although Amelia did not smoke, she also promoted Lucky Strike cigarettes. The latter were advertised as the cigarettes that were carried on

Another publicity photograph of Modernaire Earhart Luggage. The plane in the background is a Stearman C-3MB NC6488 mail plane. (Courtesy of Mary S. Lovell)

the *Friendship* flight, during which the pilot, Wilmer Stultz, and engineer, Louis Gordon, did both smoke. However, because Amelia promoted Lucky Strike cigarettes she lost her post as aviation editor for *McCall's* magazine, as society at that time viewed smoking by women as unladylike.

Amelia standing on the wheel of her Lockheed 5C Vega 'Hi-speed Special' NR965Y. (Courtesy of Mary S. Lovell)

With her sights set on new challenges Amelia knew her Lockheed Vega 5B needed a major overhaul, so she sold it, less the engine, to Philadelphia's Franklin Institute in 1933 and purchased a Lockheed 'Hi-speed Special' 5C Vega, NR965Y. The Wasp C engine that Amelia had used for her Atlantic and cross-country record flight was installed in the Vega, along with a new Hamilton Standard adjustable-pitch propeller.

Amelia also needed a technical adviser for the Pacific flight, so George approached Paul Mantz, who he had known back in 1928 when he was head of the editorial board for Paramount Pictures. Paul had a very wide experience of stunt flying and understood the latest aviation technology, so, consequently, he was invited to become Amelia's technical adviser.

Paul arranged for a two-way radio with the call sign KHABQ that transmitted on 3105 and 6210 kilocycles, and a trailing antenna and other equipment including compasses were provided. Amelia was to study the relevant maps with help from various experts in navigation.

On 26 November 1934, George, who had moved to Manhattan, telephoned Amelia to tell her that their house in Rye had caught fire and was severely damaged. A lot of its valuable contents and all the childhood memories that Amelia had saved were destroyed. George made plans to reconstruct the house and returned to California to continue with the planning for Amelia's Pacific crossing. In December, as plans for the attempt were under way, news came that another crew had been lost on the same route when Charles Ulm and his crew vanished on a test flight from Oakland to Hawaii in an Airspeed Envoy named *Stella Australis*. The crew had sent Hawaii a Morse code message saying they were lost and running out of fuel and they would have to ditch in the sea. A large, expensive search was mounted by army and navy aircraft and ships but this found nothing. It was later discovered that Ulm had not carried a life raft to save weight, believing that the aircraft would be able to float for a few days should it be forced down. Amelia would have known about the accident but remained undaunted, still determined to go ahead with her attempt.

Once all was ready, NR965Y was loaded on the foredeck of the SS *Lurline* and Amelia, George, Paul, Mrs Mantz and mechanic Ernie Tissot all boarded on 22 December to sail for Hawaii. True to form, this flight was to be kept secret and Amelia stated the trip was a lecture tour for which she would fly around the islands. This subterfuge did not last for long and once the media found out, there was condemnation of the attempt due to concerns about the expensive searches that would need to be mounted if Amelia went down in the water. There was widespread feeling this could damage the reputation of aviation.

The criticism, which also came from the NAA, continued into January 1935 and it may well have upset Amelia, but she remained steadfast. George too started to worry when sponsors threatened to pull out, but Amelia confronted them at a meeting, telling them that 'there is an aroma of cowardice in the air'. She made it clear she intended to make the flight, with or without their support. She won the battle and, although the criticism was to prove painful and disheartening for Amelia, she never wavered in her determination to carry on.

Paul was confident that the plane was ready and with 500 gallons of fuel aboard Amelia took off from

Amelia welcomed by a large crowd after the first solo flight in the NR965Y from Hawaii to California. (Courtesy of Mary S. Lovell)

Wheeler Field on 11 January, flying east over the Pacific to California. The radio telephone proved its worth and Amelia was able to maintain contact with shore stations and ships on her flight. It was not an easy trip, as she had to battle through some heavy weather and fog, but after eighteen hours sixteen minutes she landed at Oakland Airport to a large crowd that had been waiting for hours. Amelia had made it, but she was exhausted. She had originally intended to fly on to Washington DC, but knew she needed to rest.

Amelia was now the first person, man or woman, to have flown solo across both the Atlantic and Pacific oceans. She received many messages of congratulations, including one from President Roosevelt and the First Lady. This was by no means the end of her challenges as, just a few months later, Amelia met the consul general of Mexico at a reception in New York who invited her to make a goodwill visit to Mexico City, and she immediately started to make plans for a flight from California to Mexico City. George had left Paramount in March and this was an ideal time for him to focus on publicising Amelia's new venture. A postage stamp was issued by the Mexican government to commemorate the flight, and George went about organising the printing of limited edition first-day covers, which would bring in valuable funds.

On 19 April Amelia flew from California, hoping to make the 1,700-mile trip in record time, but she lost her way and had to land in Nopala, where she was redirected to Mexico City by villagers. Poor weather held up the return flight and it was not until 8 May that she was able to take off for a non-stop flight to Newark, New Jersey, making the trip in fourteen hours eighteen minutes and landing to a huge welcome by a very large crowd. Just three months later, in August, Amelia flew her Vega in the 1935 Bendix race with Paul and a mechanic on board and came in fifth, winning $500. In advance of the flight, Amelia sent George a Western Union telegram stating:

1935 AUG 29
SEYMOUR HOTEL 50 WEST 45
PAUL AND I IN BENDIX ENTERED FOR FUN SINCE SHIP ONLY STOCK MODEL HAVE ANNOUNCED WE COULD NOT STAND STRAIN WATCHING OTHERS PREPARE SO HAD TO HITCH UP OLD DOBBIN STOP PROBABLY NO RACE TONIGHT WEATHER LOVE=
A.

There had been a series of recent flying accidents and a crash in May 1935, in which Senator Bronson Cutting of New Mexico was killed, leading Congress to set up a committee to investigate airline safety. Senator Copeland of New York led the investigation and Amelia was one of those called to give evidence.

Gene Vidal, as Director of the Bureau of Air Commerce, was responsible for aviation safety and he came under considerable pressure to resign. He survived the investigation, although matters would not be easy for him in the future.

Amelia had canvassed President Franklin Roosevelt and the First Lady for Gene to be given the new role in 1933, originally as Director of the Aeronautics Branch. The name was changed to the Bureau of Air Commerce the following year.

Although George thought Amelia would now be able to spend some time in their newly rebuilt house in Rye, she was instead dashing around various cities giving lectures. She also made her first parachute jump, an

Arrival for the interview with Senator Royal S. Copeland in 1936. (National Archives)

Amelia expressing her views at the interview with Senator Royal S. Copeland. (National Archives)

A discussion between George Putnam and Gene Vidal while Amelia looks straight ahead. (Courtesy of Mary S. Lovell)

experience she shared with Gene, and then it was straight back on the lecture tour. During this punishing schedule Amelia suffered a reoccurrence of her sinus problem and had to have an operation, which led to a forced break to recuperate in Rye. Amelia longed for the warmth of the climate in California and pestered George to buy a property in Hollywood, and although he was not happy with the idea, she got her way. During this time Amelia was always thinking of what she wanted to achieve next. One possibility was a plan to go into partnership with Paul Mantz to organise various aviation projects, for which living in California would be ideal as they could meet to discuss this regularly. Another germ of an idea was the circumnavigation of the globe around the equator.

In September 1934 Amelia met Edward C. Elliott, president of Purdue University, at a conference in New York.

He was committed to the principle of educating women and ensuring they had the opportunity to forge their own careers, rather than being forced to inhabit the traditional role of the 'lady' and be expected to stay at home and look after the household. His intention was for Purdue to become a place that would give women this training and the university had established its first residence hall for women there that same year. In addition, Edward's interest in flying had led to Purdue having its own airfield, planes and hangar. It was not at all surprising that aeronautics became part of the curriculum.

Edward got to know Amelia after sitting with her at a luncheon and he was very impressed, particularly by her passionate interest in the education of women. He decided that Amelia was the type of role model he was looking for to teach at Purdue and invited her to join the staff. Edward said that she was just the person to inspire women and would like her to focus on preparing women for a modern, changing world.

With her very busy schedule, Amelia would only be able to work at Purdue for a few weeks at a time, but she was keen to be involved as much as possible. However, Amelia found that, owing to her frantic schedule, her work at Purdue became almost a period of rest. Her lectures were hugely popular and she loved the campus life and mixing with the students, who enjoyed getting to know Amelia personally instead of through what they had read about her in the press.

With her next challenge already fixed in her mind, Amelia knew she would need to replace her Vega for a more powerful aircraft and started to investigate what was available. She asked Paul to help and in November he obtained a quote for a Lockheed 10-E Electra, but

Purdue University Airport with George Putnam far left, Amelia in the centre and Edward Elliott far right. (Courtesy of Mary S. Lovell)

with the extra equipment needed for the type of trip she wanted it was possible the bill might come to more than $30,000, and that was just for the basic aircraft. With all the funds needed for the trip George was working on, the cost of an aircraft could make it more difficult to achieve. However, true to Amelia's 'lucky streak', help was not far away.

Edward was very pleased with the work she was doing and the huge impact it was having on the students at Purdue and asked if there was anything else he could do to support her work. She considered his offer and explained that she had an idea for an aircraft that could be used as a 'flying laboratory'. Edward then gained funds from the Purdue Research Foundation to purchase a brand-new Electra, as well as funds for the Amelia Earhart Fund for Aeronautical Research to develop scientific and engineering data for aeronautical development.

George had been working on the plans for the around-the-world flight, but the decision to circumnavigate the globe around the equator would mean that he would need to gain clearance to land at airports in the countries that were on the route and to also negotiate assistance from the US Navy and the Bureau of Air Commerce.

Amelia knew that other pilots had succeeded in flying around the globe, but by using the shorter route near the Arctic Circle. This was the route used by Wiley Post and his navigator, Harold Gatty, who were the first to fly around the world in 1931, and Post used the same route when he did it solo in 1933. On Sunday 11 August 1935, Amelia and George visited Will Rogers at his ranch in Santa Monica. Also present was Post, who with Rogers was preparing to leave on an around-the-world flight. Just four days later they were killed when their plane, *Winnie Mae*, stalled following engine trouble on take-off and crashed near Port Barrow, Alaska. This loss of her friends upset Amelia, but she was well aware that she risked her life every time she went into the air. She kept her sadness hidden and immersed herself in giving a lecture in Lakeside, Ohio, before returning to California.

The round-the-equator route Amelia had chosen had never been attempted before; it was much longer than the Arctic Circle route and there was the possibility of even greater danger and more hazards, especially when having to cross the entire Pacific Ocean, but it remained her choice. She was aware of the risks but was set on making it another of her 'firsts'.

The order was placed for the Electra, which was powered by two 550hp Pratt & Whitney R-1340 Wasp engines, giving it a maximum speed of just over 200mph. The cabin space usually used for passenger seats held additional fuel tanks for 753 gallons and the wing fuel tanks held 398 gallons. There was also a roof hatch for navigation, and this equipment included two magnetic compasses, a Bendix radio direction finder, a Western Electric two-way radio and microphone system capable of transmitting on 500, 3105 and 6210kcs, and a Sperry autopilot system. The Electra was given the registration number NR16020. After being test flown by Lockheed's test pilot, Elmer C. McLeod, the plane was delivered on 24 July, her birthday.

The next important stage for Amelia was for her to learn to fly a more complex aircraft, so she and Paul flew up and down the west coast until she felt more comfortable. Paul was not happy with her progress and insisted that she practiced learning instrument flying in a link trainer in his hangar in Burbank. In the end, Paul was not convinced Amelia would be able to master the flying of the complex controls of the Electra, no matter how much she practiced. It was a difficult thing for him to admit, as he had a great respect for Amelia, but deep down he was worried.

The Purdue University Lockheed Vega 10-E 'Flying Laboratory'.
(Courtesy of Bill Larkin's Collection)

In August, Amelia, Paul and mechanic 'Bo' McNeely flew the Electra from Burbank to Floyd Bennett Field, New York, where she wanted to test the Electra in the Bendix race back to Los Angeles.

Amelia by this time was quite comfortable financially and maintained regular financial support for her mother, Amy, and help for her sister, Muriel, and her family. For her own travel comfort, Amelia bought a Cord 812 Westchester sedan car.

On 4 September 1936, women came to the fore again when the Cleveland to Los Angeles Bendix race was won by Louise Thaden and Blanche Noyes flying a Beechcraft C-17R, followed by Laura Ingalls flying solo, who took second place. Amelia had taken off, with Helen Richey as co-pilot. It was an extremely uncomfortable flight, as the cockpit hatch flew open, to the shock of both pilots, who almost got sucked out of the plane. After a few hours they succeded in jamming the hatch closed and managed to finish, beating some of the men and discovering with pride that the women had done very well. This was the first time since the Bendix Trophy race began in 1931 that women flyers had won.

Helen Richey had gained her pilot's licence in 1930 and became well known for being the co-pilot for Frances Marsalis when they set up a record for a ten-day endurance flight in January 1934. Sadly, Frances was killed in August 1934 during the Cleveland Air Races. Helen became the first woman to fly a commercial airliner when she accepted a position with Central Airlines in December 1934. In 1942 she became a wartime aircraft ferry pilot when she joined the British Air Transport Auxiliary (ATA).

There was also another 'first' on 4 September 1936; this time it was not down to Amelia, but to British-born Beryl

Amelia standing in front of her Cord 812 Westchester sedan, with the Lockheed Vega in the background. (Courtesy of Mary S. Lovell)

Amelia standing in front of hangars 4 and 5 at Oakland's Old North Field Airport with her Cord automobile. As Amelia only had one Cord it seems that she had side mirrors fitted, as in other photographs no such mirrors are visible. (Courtesy of Jim Geldert Collection)

Markham, who became the first woman to fly east to west from England to North America. She took off from Abingdon, Oxfordshire, for New York in her Vega Gull VP-KCC *The Messenger* and flew for twenty-one hours thirty-five minutes. Her flight ended when carburettor ice problems forced her to crash-land in a peat bog on Cape Breton Island, Nova Scotia. Amelia, having been the first woman to fly the Atlantic west to east in 1932, professed herself 'delighted that Mrs. Markham should have succeeded in her exploit'.

In late September, Amelia flew the Electra from California to Purdue University in Lafayette, Indiana, with husband George and mechanic 'Bo' McKneely, who were passengers. Amelia was the only pilot flying the aircraft and had to contend with a much heavier plane with two powerful engines and retractable landing gear, something she had not been used to. Late in October she began a week-long trip back to California, sharing the cockpit with Jacqueline Cochran.

Jacqueline was an aviation pioneer, widely considered to be one of the most skilled pilots of her time, winning five Harmon Trophies for being the most outstanding woman pilot in the world. She set a new speed record in 1937 and won the 1938 Los Angeles to Cleveland Bendix race. She was later known as the 'Speed Queen'. In the Second World War she worked for the ATA, recruiting qualified American women pilots to join in Britain.

5

AROUND-THE-WORLD ATTEMPT ONE

OAKLAND TO HONOLULU

In preparation for the around-the-world flight, Amelia trained herself like an athlete. Her sister, Muriel, was a witness to some of this and commented, 'She trained very definitely to stay awake if need be from 18 hours of a stretch, and she trained herself on tomato juice and different things, in order to be able to undergo the same type of rigorous exercise that the man would.'

This training was essential because many of the flight legs were very long and as Amelia was the only pilot she would have to remain awake and alert from take-off to landing. Her diet would need to be controlled, although, as Amelia said, there was often not much need for food because of the concentration required to fly, although liquids would have been necessary to avoid dehydration.

As the aim was to follow the equator, there would have to be refuelling and maintenance points on the route. This would be important after flying from Oakland to Honolulu due to the long crossing to Australia and there

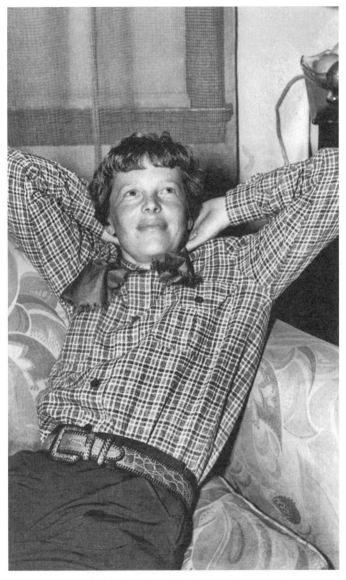

Along with all the preparations and training for her around-the-world flight, Amelia made sure she relaxed at her Oakland home. (Oakland Air Museum Collection)

would be a problem finding points for refuelling on such a large expanse of water. This was one of the issues with which George had to contend.

The arrangements for the flight included getting everything in place for the various refuelling stops, including spare parts and organising the use of mechanics for servicing the plane. George would also have to gain permission for overflying every country, as well as for the landings for refuelling and maintenance where this was to take place. He would also have to go to the government authorities to gain information on charts and weather data over the Pacific.

The problem of refilling the fuel tanks in the Pacific was complicated, but it was possible that this could be carried out by aerial refuelling. The navy was agreeable to this providing Amelia had special training, but there would be a cost to her. This would not just be a financial cost, but also one of fatigue. If she was to refuel in the air it would mean flying for at least twenty-four hours to complete the distance across the Pacific. However, it was Gene Vidal who came up with a solution. There were many small islands in the South Pacific and one in particular was Howland Island, just 2 miles long by ½ a mile wide, standing just a few feet above the Pacific. It was 1,800 miles south-west of Honolulu and an island on which the United States wanted to establish a permanent presence. Gene had begun by getting groups of students from the Kamehameha School for Boys, which was a private school in Honolulu, to study the island environment. There were four groups of students, which were rotated every three months, and they had been told they were part of a scientific expedition studying the island. What they did not know was that there was a plan to develop a landing strip that would act as a stopover for commercial flights from the United States to Australia, a project that in 1937 had received the full approval of President Roosevelt. Gradually others arrived aboard the US Coast Guard cutter SS *Itasca* and a settlement was built up of wood-framed living quarters and tents, which were named 'Itascatown'. These teams were tasked to conduct hourly weather observations.

A decision was made to create an airfield on Howland Island, with the project being administered by three authorities: the Works Progress Administration (WPA), Interior Department and the Bureau for Air Commerce, of which Gene was director.

Gene believed that Howland Island was in a good position for Amelia's route from Honolulu and an ideal place for building a landing strip and storing the fuel needed for the Electra when it landed there. He thus went about arranging the building work.

WPA workmen, along with their two heavy tractors and other equipment, left Honolulu on 13 January 1937 for Howland Island aboard the US Coast Guard cutter *Duane*. Also on board was Robert M. Campbell, divisional inspector of airports, Richard B. Black, Department of the Interior, and several army and navy officers.

The next important job for George was to look for the professional help required for the flight, and Clarence S. Williams, a navy navigator, was to prepare the charts for the whole route, although the traditional ones were old and inaccurate for the area in the Pacific that Amelia's route was to cross. The US Navy had carried out recent work to correct the charts and Clarence would be well placed to get access to them, but unfortunately they were classified. Amelia wrote a personal letter to President Roosevelt asking for his help, the result of which was his support and approval, which he passed on to the Chief of the Naval Operations to action.

Another trusted friend was Albert Bresnik, who was at the time a photographer for CBS. He was approached by George and taken on as Amelia's personal photographer in 1932 because she was tired of having her pictures taken by different people. Albert was an experienced photographer who had spent many years in Hollywood, and he got on very well with Amelia. They joked a lot in the photo sessions and he remarked that she called him 'her little brother', trusting him with her personal thoughts.

It was originally planned for Albert to accompany Amelia and her team to take photographs on the first flight, but this did not happen in the end. At first Amelia only intended to have one crew member, Captain Harry Manning, who

Clarence Williams, Harry Manning and Amelia study the maps that Clarence had prepared for the around-the-world flight. (Courtesy of Mary S. Lovell)

was to be the navigator/radio operator across the Pacific Ocean section from Oakland to Australia. Amelia already knew Harry as he was the master of the SS *President Roosevelt* that carried the *Friendship* crew back to the USA after their historic Atlantic flight, and he had taken leave of absence from the shipping line to be involved in Amelia's project. The intention was for Harry to navigate the Pacific Ocean route and Amelia was going to fly solo from then on, but she reconsidered this plan because she could see the difficulty of Harry also having to serve as radio operator. Paul, who was responsible for giving technical advice for the flight, suggested she brought in the highly experienced Fred Noonan as navigator, as he had worked on Pan American Clipper flying boats and knew the San Francisco to Honolulu route well. However, there was just one problem

Amelia Earhart and Captain Harry Manning, her navigator, check instruments in the plane to be used on the world flight. It was first intended that Harry would navigate for Amelia across the Pacific to Australia, but that was later changed to include Fred Noonan as navigator. Paul Mantz was in charge of technical matters. (Courtesy of Mary S. Lovell)

with this appointment, and it was one that Amelia needed to consider carefully: it was well known in flying circles that Fred was a heavy drinker. Despite his reputation as a highly experienced navigator, could he be trusted to be responsible to navigate such an important mission? With Amelia's childhood experience of her father's drinking habits, it was ironic that she should place her trust in Fred for the world flight. That was Amelia, as unpredictable as ever.

The landing strip on Howland Island was almost finished and the navy and coastguard ship were getting into position for Amelia's take-off from Oakland. However, the weather was not suitable until 17 March, when conditions were just right. Late in the afternoon, Amelia, Paul, Harry and Fred took off bound for Hawaii. Paul only intended to go as far as Honolulu, but as it was a tiring journey Amelia passed the controls over to Paul to land there. The Electra

Left to right: Paul Mantz, Amelia, Harry Manning and Fred Noonan. (Courtesy of Mary S. Lovell)

had set a new speed record of fifteen hours forty-seven minutes. The Electra was checked over and made ready for the next stage of the world flight, but Amelia noticed that Fred was drinking heavily again and considered taking him off the attempt.

By 20 March she had reassessed the problem and decided to carry on with two navigators. Amelia and the crew got into the Electra and took up their positions. Harry was at the chart table in the cabin and Fred was in the co-pilot's seat alongside Amelia as she started the engines and prepared to take off down the paved runway at Luke Field on Ford Island, Pearl Harbour. As she built up speed, the plane suddenly started to swerve to the right, so Amelia reduced the power on the opposite engine. The plane then started to swing from the right to the left and then ground looped, with the undercarriage collapsing, then skidding along the ground with sparks flying and fuel spraying out. This was also confirmed by eyewitnesses; however, some observers thought the accident was caused by a tyre bursting, but experienced aviators stated that it was human error and blamed Amelia for her steering of the aircraft.

The attempt on the world flight had ended before it had barely begun, but fortunately there were no injuries to the crew and they all climbed out of the aircraft. Amelia, who was much shaken, was relieved that no one was injured and indicated to Paul, who was duly concerned, that she thought a shock absorber might have given way.

Paul had reminded Amelia constantly to use the rudder pedals to keep the plane straight and to push both throttles together smoothly, and not, as was her practice, to increase power in the opposite engine to keep straight. Ignoring this advice could lead to a ground loop, but it appeared Amelia had not realised its importance.

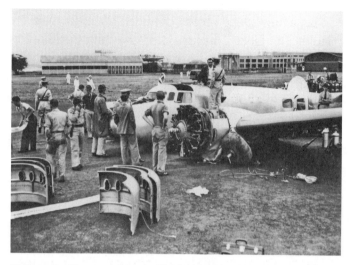

The result of the crash at Luke Field, when the plane ground looped. Paul Mantz can be seen in the hatchway. (Courtesy of Mary S. Lovell)

Art Kennedy refers to this incident in his book *High Times Keeping 'em Flying*. Art was a mechanic who had worked on Amelia's planes from 1930–37 and saw the damaged aircraft when it arrived at Pacific Airmotive Company (PAC). He commented that an air accident investigator hinted that he thought it was a faked ground loop made to look like an accident. In the book Art said to Amelia, 'What's going on here? This couldn't have been a normal ground loop. It was forced. Why?' He was told quietly by Amelia to mind his own business and not mention it. When Art told her the inspector was to arrive the next day and referred to the collapsed landing gear in the wrong position to the turn of the ground loop, Amelia said, 'Art, you and I are good friends. You didn't see a thing. We'll just force the gear back over to make it look natural. Will you promise never to say anything about what you know?'

Art and his wife, Polly, became very close to Amelia and had private conversations with her. They promised never to say anything about what he knew. He comments in his book, 'I said, "Sure Amelia", and I kept that promise for fifty years.'

This accident did not deter Amelia, who had already decided that she would try again as soon as the plane had been returned to Burbank and repaired. After telephoning George in Oakland and explaining what had happened, Amelia, along with Paul, Harry and Fred, boarded the *Malolo* and left Hawaii to sail to Los Angeles.

George then set about making arrangements for the Electra to be shipped to Los Angeles for repair, but as the plane was uninsured it would be a heavy drain on the family savings. Friends would give them support, but Amelia was philosophical in her statement: 'I more or less mortgaged my future.' She added, 'Without regret, however, for what are futures for?'

6

AROUND-THE-WORLD ATTEMPT TWO

OAKLAND TO NATAL

Following the accident at Luke Field and the many media reports and critical statements made by experienced aviators, Amelia had to endure a period of attack on her reputation, but she stubbornly soldiered on. Amelia would never give in when she had her back against the wall, it only made her more determined to fight on and try and try again until she succeeded. This was her attitude to the second attempt at an around-the-world flight, but fate decreed she would not succeed this time.

Harry's leave of absence was coming to an end and he had to return to his ship. At the time he praised Amelia for cutting the switches to avoid a fire when they crashed. However, years later he was to state that one of his reasons for going back to his ship and not asking for an extension of his leave was because he had little faith in Amelia's flying ability and her tough nature left their working relationship quite strained at times.

Paul had become aware of Amelia growing increasingly distant from him, despite his working solidly on various tasks while the plane was being repaired to help her with her world flight. Once the plane had been returned, Amelia and Paul flew to Oakland for a test run, where Amelia said, 'Our friend Elmer Dimity quietly slipped on board the cargo of "covers" carried for philatelists.' These first covers had been carried on the first attempt when they landed in Honolulu and were intended to raise a substantial amount of cash to fund the flight. Paul was more concerned that he had not been able to make the final checks on the radio and on the fuel consumption for each leg of the flight to ensure Amelia knew the best power settings. Joseph Gurr, who came to check the radio, felt Amelia was paying too little attention to the proper use of it as well as to other safety issues. He suggested that he should give her a course of instruction on the radio and the direction-finding equipment, specifically in tuning, operation of the transmitter, and how to take a bearing using the direction finder. However, due to her busy schedule, Amelia left after an hour, saying she had a pre-arranged appointment. Joseph said that he did not have time to show her how to take a bearing with the direction finder, or to ensure she knew all that was required for contacting other radio stations.

Further concerns were raised after Harry had left when Amelia had the Morse code equipment and long trailing antenna removed because he had been the only one able to use it. Although there was a concern over weight, it was also because Amelia and Fred had little confidence in their skills for using the Morse code system and saw themselves as 'amateurs'. On reflection, it might have been

Amelia and Fred Noonan in the hangar at the Panamanian Flying Field, Natal. (Courtesy of Mary S. Lovell)

prudent for either Fred or Amelia, or both, to have taken a crash course on Morse to use in case of emergencies. There was also concern over their knowledge of voice transmission. Amelia only had one hour's instruction on how to use the plane's radio equipment; it was not a good omen for the future.

Furthermore, a lack of trust appeared to be developing between Amelia and Paul, causing him to get very frustrated. This became clear to Paul when Amelia told him she would be spending some days in Burbank for pre-flight preparations and he fully expected to be consulted, but was not.

On the second attempt it would only be Amelia as pilot and Fred as navigator. As it was planned for later in the year, they would be running into changing world weather conditions. To avoid Asia's monsoon season the decision was made to reverse the original route and fly eastwards instead. The biggest problem was the long flight across the Pacific Ocean from Lae, New Guinea, to the tiny Howland Island. By that time they would both be very tired, but Fred would still be expected to hit the island spot on using celestial navigation.

This change in flight plan saw George once again embroiled in getting clearances from all the countries, but this was made more difficult because Gene had resigned as Director of the Bureau of Air Commerce, which meant George no longer had inside help with the various government authorities with which he wished to negotiate. Further support was given by a friend, Jacques de Sibour, who was able to help George in gaining the necessary permissions.

Amelia had begun work on her book, *Last Flight*, and once she started the flight she intended to keep notes that would be sent back to George, mailed from each stopping off point, which she planned to use once the challenge was over to help complete the book.

Amelia was impatient to make a start on the attempt and with the plane ready and all necessary arrangements completed, she left Oakland for Miami on 21 May 1937, with George, Fred and Lockheed mechanic 'Bo' McKneely as passengers. Amelia intended to use this flight as a shake-down flight to see if there were any problems that might need fixing. They stopped off at Tucson, Arizona, and while taxiing to take on fuel one of the engines burst into flames, but was quickly put out and the engine cleaned up. The next morning they took off for New Orleans in the midst of a sandstorm and then flew over the Gulf of Mexico to Tampa and then on to Miami, arriving on 23 May. The Electra went in for its final checks with Pan

Amelia and George saying their final goodbye before take-off on the second around-the-world attempt. Although they maintained contact for most of the flight to Lae, they would never meet again. (Courtesy of Mary S. Lovell)

American mechanics before Amelia and Fred left for the around-the-world trip. While waiting at Miami, George wrote about information on the departure of the Electra for the *New York Herald Tribune*.

On 1 June, Amelia, George and Fred arrived at 5.30 a.m. at Miami Airport, where they were met by a crowd of a few hundred well-wishers waiting to watch Electra NR16020 take off. Amelia and George said their private goodbyes while holding hands and then it was time for her and Fred to climb into the Electra. A short while after warming the engines, the Electra took off with a course set for a crossing of the Caribbean to San Juan, Puerto Rico. In her book Amelia describes the trip and what could be seen from the air. Around forty minutes out, she saw the Bahama Banks and also commented on a submerged wreck seen while flying at a 1,000ft. She was feeling very laid back when she commented, 'What with such expert navigational help and the Sperry gyropilot, I began to feel that my long-range flying was becoming pretty sissy.' At about noon Amelia was told by Fred that they were too far south, so she changed course as directed and soon after sighted Puerto Rico. They followed the shoreline until they saw the airport near to the city of Don Juan, where it had been arranged for them to stay at the estate of pilot Clara Livingston, and prepared to land.

The next leg of the journey was from Don Juan to Paramaribo, Dutch Guiana. It was a pleasant moment for Amelia when she sighted the coast of Venezuela and, in her words, 'As we drew near I saw the densely wooded mountains and between them wide valleys of open plains and jungle. I had never seen a jungle before.' They landed at Caripito, Venezuela, where the airport was jointly managed by Pan American Airways and the Standard Oil Company.

This was where the Electra was to be refuelled while Amelia and Fred were entertained as guests at a luncheon. They left the next morning and later sighted Georgetown, British Guiana, before flying directly over thick jungle while heading for Paramaribo, where they landed for the Electra to be oiled and refuelled. Amelia and Fred had an hour's railway journey into Paramaribo, where they stayed in comfort at the Palace Hotel. They were delayed for one day because of the weather and then it was back to the Electra to take off for Fortaleza, Brazil. While at Fortaleza the facilities of Pan American Airways were used to prepare for the South Atlantic crossing from Natal, which was just 270 miles from Fortaleza.

The next morning they took off at 4.50 a.m. and arrived at Natal at 6.55 a.m., which was a short journey compared to some they had made, as Amelia commented, 'So our day's work was done almost before conventional breakfast time.' The airport at Natal was used by a number of international flights, and whilst the plane was being refuelled, Amelia began to consider how she would fly the South Atlantic. The South Atlantic crossing had been made by Air France for a number of years, with two flights a week just carrying mail, so Amelia met the crew of the next flight out and was able to get some valuable advice from them. They told her they preferred to fly very early because they expected the most difficult weather during the first 800 miles. This was good advice and Amelia decided to act upon it, planning to leave early the next morning.

Their take-off from Natal for Dakar was at 3.15 a.m. in darkness and was thought by Amelia to be 'uneventful except for little incidents of long-range flying'. There was a variation in weather conditions, with clear sky followed by heavy rain squalls, and at 6.50 a.m. they crossed the equator at 6,000ft. They passed an Air France mail plane but could not communicate because, as Amelia states, 'The mail plane's radio equipment, I believe is telegraphic, while mine, at the moment was exclusively voice telephone.'

On approaching the African coastline, no position sighting was possible because of thick haze. However, when Fred told Amelia to turn south, she decided instead that a 'left turn' was the best and after 50 miles flying north up the coast they arrived at St Louis, Senegal. Had Amelia followed Fred's instruction they would have arrived at Dakar within thirty minutes.

The next day was 8 June and they flew the 163 miles from St Louis to Dakar and stayed a day there to have a fuel meter replaced that had broken just after leaving Natal. They were well looked after in Dakar, staying at the mansion of the governor general and also entertained at a reception given by the Aero Club. While the Electra was being serviced by Air France mechanics, Amelia and Fred rested before they started the long air route across Africa.

CENTRAL AFRICA, INDIAN SUBCONTINENT AND ASIA LEG

For their next stage of the journey the weather reports were not very encouraging, with the possibility of tornadoes through their planned route. Amelia had originally intended to fly to Niamey, but on advice she decided to change her course and fly the 1,140 miles to Gao. The flight took them inland, flying at 150mph crossing the River Senegal and later the upper reaches of the River Niger, finally landing at Gao after a flight of seven hours

Refuelling the plane in Africa. This was quite a difficult task because the fuel had to be siphoned from drums and filtered before entering the fuel tanks. At every refuelling stop either Amelia or Fred would supervise to make sure the task was done correctly. (Courtesy of Mary S. Lovell)

fifty minutes. The Electra was taken into a hangar and the mechanics started checking her and refuelling from the 50-gallon drums that had been allotted to Amelia months before, and which had her name printed on them.

After a night's rest, Amelia and Fred prepared for the next stage of their journey, from Gao to Fort Lamy, but it was not so easy for Fred to navigate across this stretch of Africa due to the inaccuracy of many of the maps. They were held up at Fort Lamy until later in the day because of a small leak in a shock absorber in the landing gear. Due to the lateness of the flight, they made for El Fasher, where they landed and were welcomed by Governor Ingallson and his wife. They were to stay with them in the former sultan's palace and Amelia was amused because her room was next door to what would have previously been the harem.

The next day they took off to fly the 500 miles from El Fasher to Khartoum, where they landed and refuelled. Within two hours they were on their way again, this time to Massawa to allow the mechanics, none of whom spoke English, to get on with the work on the Electra. They stayed the night in Italian army quarters, but were relieved when an English-speaking officer asked Amelia if she was hungry, which she was, having not eaten anything the whole day.

It was now 14 June and the next flight was down the Red Sea from Massawa to Assab in preparation for their next long flight along the Arabian coast to India. The next day they left Assab early, but flying over Arabia was not easy to organise because of the reluctance of Arabia to allow foreign planes to fly over the region. Due to the Electra's ability to fly non-stop to India without having to make a forced landing on Arabian sand, permission to make the flight was given; however, the flight was also helped by the British, who gave permission to land at Aden and then to fly on to Karachi. The 1,920-mile flight from Assab to Karachi took thirteen hours ten minutes, and once they had landed they were met by Jacques de Sibour, who told Amelia there was a phone call for her. Thinking it would be from a media organisation, she was surprised to learn it was George on the line. They discussed the flight and Amelia told him she was fine and that she would soon see him in Oakland. In Karachi Amelia found time to experience her first camel ride and was warned by the owner that her camel was a naughty one. After the ride she said she was convinced that camels should have shock absorbers. While in Karachi the Electra was worked on by Imperial Airways mechanics to get her ready for the next part of the journey.

They left Karachi on 17 June to fly the 1,390 miles to Calcutta, where they finally landed at Dum Dum aerodrome just after 4 p.m. It was an interesting flight and just before landing at the aerodrome they came into heavy rain, but were able to land safely. The mechanics then began their work on the Electra while Amelia and Fred travelled by car to stay with their host for the night.

They returned to the airport at dawn and took off for Akyab over farming country before arriving over the airfield, which had two runways and a large hangar and was used regularly by the Dutch airline KLM, Air France and Imperial Airways. This was just a brief stop for refuelling and a weather check before flying on to Rangoon. After taking off again they ran into monsoon conditions, which made flying very difficult, so they decided to return to Akyab. Amelia was amazed at the way in which Fred, who could not see anything but the waves below the plane, still managed to navigate safely.

The next day, 19 June, they took off from Akyab and planned to fly to Bangkok, but were not given permission to do so, landing instead at Rangoon, just 400 miles from Akyab. This was not a good flight, as the weather was worse than the day before, but Amelia managed to land safely. However, the weather on arrival was so bad that they decided to stay over in Rangoon before flying on to Bangkok. After having a sightseeing tour they were invited to stay at the American consul's home for the night before leaving Rangoon for Bangkok, where they refuelled. They then took off again, this time for Singapore, a flight of more than 900 miles. Amelia comments in her book, 'Along that day's route I was interested to see charming towns, which looked from the air much like those at home.' They landed at Singapore to be welcomed by the American consul general, who had arranged to put them up for the night. Amelia said, 'I explained our disagreeable habit of getting up at three in the morning and falling asleep immediately after dinner.'

After taking off the next day from Singapore, they headed for Java, crossing the equator for the third time while flying over small islands, beautiful countryside, jungles and mountains and finally landing in Bandung. While KLM mechanics checked the Electra, Amelia had a telephone call from New York. They dined at one of KLM's pilot's homes before checking in at a hotel. It was while in Bandung that Amelia fell ill and, combined with the lack of sleep, appeared utterly worn out. Amelia was desperately in need of some sustained rest, but, as ever, she was determined to press on. Before she took off on her previous flight Amelia had confided in Alfred Breznak, her personal photographer, in her kitchen and told him that she thought she might be pregnant. Her logged reports on the flight mention her being sick in the mornings, so it is a reasonable supposition that she might have been suffering from morning sickness.

The next morning they were told that a mechanic had discovered a faulty instrument and their departure would have to wait until a replacement was found. It was later in the day before they could take off to fly the 350 miles to Surabaya, but once in the air they found that the instruments needed further adjustments and they returned to Bandung – it was important that these problems were dealt with by skilled mechanics to avoid future hazards. While waiting they did some sightseeing, but it was not until Sunday 27 June that they finally left Bandung, this time for Port Darwin, but they had to land at Kupang on Timor Island to stay the night at a government rest house, after which they left Kupang and crossed the Timor Sea to Port Darwin, Australia.

From Port Darwin it was a flight of seven hours forty-three minutes to Lae, New Guinea, arriving on 30 June. Amelia described the landing field at Lae as one long strip cut out of the jungle, ending abruptly on a cliff at the water's edge. 'It is 3,000 feet long and firm under all conditions. There are hangars, but a number of planes have to be hitched outside. I noticed all these were metal ones. In regular service here is another Electra, sister to my own.' The total miles Amelia and Fred had covered was 22,000 and they had another 7,000 to go, flying across the Pacific Ocean for their arrival back at Oakland, California.

After arriving at Lae the Electra was serviced, fuelled and oiled to capacity ready for their longest flight of 2,556 miles to Howland Island. The photographs taken in Lae showed Amelia and Fred looking physically exhausted and in dire need of rest and relaxation before taking to the air again. However, even then Amelia made an effort to put on her captivating smile.

Amelia wanted to take off again on 1 July for the flight to Howland, then on to Honolulu, before arriving back at Oakland, California, on 4 July, but was keenly aware that the next stage would be physically demanding. Fred spent some of his time trying to set his chronometers, but at first had difficulties with the radio equipment. Fortunately this problem was resolved, but as Howland Island was just a small dot in the Pacific, every navigational aid was essential for successfully pinpointing the island. Amelia and Fred spent 30 June repacking the plane and removing all unwanted, inessential items to reduce the weight in the plane, but that was not strictly the case, as confirmed by Harry Balfour, the radio operator at

Lae. He said that even some of the important survival equipment, including the Very pistol and flares to send distress signals, was taken off. Amelia had earlier taken off the parachutes because she considered they would be of little use while flying over the wide expanse of the Pacific Ocean, though it appears that the life rafts were still on board and well stocked with food, as well as an orange kite. On reflection, these aforementioned items should have been considered essential because there are many small islands in the Pacific, and in a scenario whereby the plane developed serious problems and there was a need to evacuate, the parachutes could have been used to drop onto any islands that might have been in the area. In addition, the Very pistol and flares could have been used for sending up distress signals, whether from land or from a life raft.

Amelia looking extremely exhausted at Lae before taking off on the flight to Howland Island. (Courtesy of Mary S. Lovell)

That night Amelia and Fred had a disagreement after which he got very drunk on whisky, causing great concern to Amelia as she had planned to leave on 1 July. She knew it was essential that Fred was at his best if they were to reach Howland Island. She decided to cancel the flight for another twenty-four hours, giving her an opportunity to keep an eye on Fred and ensure he was not drinking again before the next day's flight.

FINAL LEG BEFORE DISAPPEARING

Amelia was getting increasingly anxious and keenly wanted to take off for Howland Island. Everything was ready and the plane was fuelled up to maximum. At 00.00 hours GMT (Greenwich Mean Time), which was 10 a.m. local time at Lae on Friday 2 July, Amelia and Fred set off from Lae for Howland Island. The take-off was interesting, if not a little frightening, when they started off down the long 3,000ft runway towards the cliff with a 25ft drop at the end. As the plane left the ground it was just a matter of feet away from the cliff end, disappearing from view due to its heavy weight. All those watching were relieved when the plane came back into view while climbing, after flying just a few feet above the waves and throwing up spray from the propellers. Those watching from the airfield included pilots of Guinea Airways, who were impressed with Amelia's handling of the plane, especially as it was carrying such a heavy weight of fuel.

Once in the air, Amelia set the compass heading direct for Howland Island and Fred calculated they should arrive in eighteen hours. The fact that they left at 00.00 GMT made it easier to work out their position from the celestial sights, for now Fred's watch time and GMT were the same. Using this method, it did not matter which time zones or meridians they may have crossed as 17.45 hours GMT would mean they would have been in the air for seventeen hours forty-five minutes. With this all in place, Fred was confident he could successfully navigate to Howland Island.

It was going to be a long and difficult flight for both Amelia and Fred, with the important role they each had to perform. Amelia would be seated at the pilot's seat in the cabin (which she had described as 4ft 6in by 4ft 6in, with 4ft 8in headroom, for the entire estimated eighteen-hour flight to Howland Island) while Fred would be working at the chart table that was 18in from the ground and poorly lit. Amelia would be unable to get out of the pilot's seat to stretch her legs, unless the conditions were right for her to use the autopilot. Fred could stand slightly but he had little room to stretch his legs. It was also a very lonely existence for both due to the continuous noise from the engines; most of the communication was done with notes passed over a pulley system using a fishing line.

For the first part of the flight Amelia was to maintain contact with Harry Balfour, the Guinea Airways radio operator at Lae, with a schedule of receiving on the hour and half hour and transmitting fifteen and forty-five minutes past each hour. Not long after Amelia left Lae, she started sending voice messages using her call letters KHAQQ. However, it appeared that she was unable to receive return calls, making it impossible to establish any form of two-way communication. Balfour attempted to report the stronger headwinds to Amelia by radio on each hour for three hours, but it is not known whether or not she received those messages because no acknowledgements were received.

It was not until 05.00 hours GMT (3 p.m. local time Lae) that a call was made by Amelia, Earhart to Lae: 'At 10,000 ft but reducing altitude because of banks of cumulus cloud.' Then at 07.00 hours GMT (5 p.m. local time), Earhart to Lae: 'At 7,000 ft and making 150 mph.' This was followed shortly after at 07.20 hours GMT (5.20 p.m. local time), Earhart to Lae: 'Position Latitude: 4 degrees 33.5' South, Longitude: 159 degrees 07' East', which showed that she was approximately 20 miles south-west of the Nukumanu Islands and proved that Fred was navigating perfectly on their planned course. The last message with Balfour was very faint and was at 08.00 hours GMT (6 p.m. local time), Earhart to Lae: 'On course for Howland Island at 12,000 ft.' Then Balfour was informed by Amelia that she was changing from her daytime frequency of 6,210kcs to her night-time frequency of 3,105kcs. Balfour asked her to stay on her present frequency, but Amelia said she wanted to make contact with the US Coast Guard cutter *Itasca*.

The *Itasca* was standing off Howland Island and the coal-burning tug USS *Ontario* was positioned between New Guinea and the island to stay in radio contact with Amelia should she need assistance. However, the USS *Ontario* was not equipped with high-frequency radio so could not receive any transmissions on 3105kcs or 6210kcs, and her low-frequency radio only allowed communication with its base in Samoa at night, thus causing a twenty-four-hour delay.

Captain Harry Manning had been concerned when he was navigator that Amelia had decided she was only going to use the 3,105 and 6,210kcs bands. The Electra was using the Western Electric radio system, which was capable of transmitting on 500, 3,105 and 6,210kcs. To Harry, the 500kcs band was the standard frequency used by most ships and he saw it as the most important of all the frequencies for her to use when flying over the Pacific. It would be the ships and shore stations that used this waveband that would be Amelia's main source of radio assistance during this part of her flight. Harry had known how useful the shore-based stations were, and on the flight to Honolulu had held down the Morse code key to enable the shore-based direction finder to take a bearing on them. However, both Captain Manning and Commander Thompson of the *Itasca* were unaware that Amelia could not communicate on 500kcs because the 250 trailing antenna needed for that frequency, along with the Morse key, had been left behind in the USA. Furthermore, it was discovered by Elgen Long's research that the Western Electric system fitted by Joe Gurr had been replaced in Miami with the new Bendix RA-1 system.

At 10.30 hours GMT (8 p.m. local time) Amelia was picked up by Nauru Radio when she broadcast, 'A ship in sight ahead,' but no two-way communication was achieved, although the message was also picked up by some Nauru listeners on their short-wave radios.

Itasca had been sending Morse code messages for hours to help guide Amelia to Howland Island, but the ship was not sure if she was receiving their messages. However, at 14.15 hours GMT (2.45 a.m. local time) Amelia made contact with the *Itasca* on 3,105kcs. Her voice was very faint and they could just make out 'cloudy and overcast'. It was getting very tense in *Itasca's* radio room while all were listening intensely to the loudspeaker. Those present included chief radioman Leo G. Bellarts and two assistant radiomen, Commander Thompson, *Itasca's* captain, plus three of his officers. There was also Richard Black from the Department of the Interior and two agency reporters from Associated Press and United Press.

At 15.15 hours GMT (3.45 a.m. local time) Amelia was heard to broadcast, 'Overcast, will listen on hour and half-hour on 3,105.' The strength of the signal was better and the message was heard clearly by all in the radio room. (Signal strengths are recorded in five strengths from very weak to very strong. For example: Strength 1 very weak, Strength 2 weak, Strength 3 moderate, Strength 4 strong and Strength 5 very strong.)

There was no signal from Amelia at 15.45 hours GMT (4.15 a.m. local time). *Itasca* tried to make contact at 16.00 hours GMT (4.30 a.m. local time) but had had no response by 16.15 hours GMT. Bellarts waited a few minutes and then sent a weather report on 3,105 by voice and by Morse code. There was what appeared to be a transmission from Amelia shortly after at strength 1, but only the words 'partly cloudy' could be made out. However, the *Itasca* continued sending the weather reports while asking Amelia for her position for almost an hour and a half.

At 17.44 hours GMT (6.14 a.m. local time) *Itasca* received a message: 'This is KHAQQ ... want bearing on 3015 ... on hour ... will whistle in mike.' Then, one minute later, at 17.45 hours GMT (6.15 a.m. local time) and dawn at Howland Island, a message came in, 'About two hundred miles out ... approx ... whistling now.' This signal was at strength 3, but it was not helpful to the *Itasca's* radio team as it was not long enough for them to plot it with the direction finder. At 18.00 hours GMT (6.30 a.m. local time) a further message was sent to Amelia from *Itasca* giving a weather report and asking for her position.

At 18.15 hours GMT (6.45 a.m. local time) Amelia transmitted a message that was strength 4, 'Please take bearing on us and report in half hour ... I will make noise in microphone ... about 100 miles out.' Again, the message was too short to take a bearing, but it was an encouraging sign that the signal strength was at strength 4 with the messages much louder, indicating that the plane was getting nearer.

At 18.48 hours GMT (7.18 a.m. local time) there was a message sent from *Itasca*, 'Cannot take bearing on 3105 very good … please send on 500 or do you wish to take bearings on us … go ahead please.'

The master of the *Itasca* decided that, as they were unable to get a bearing on the plane, it was time to start making plumes of black smoke with a hope that it would be visible for at least 20 miles. If that was identified by Amelia she could then set her course to land at Howland Island. The problem was that the black plume of smoke tended to blow away over the surface of the sea and quickly thinned out, which would have made it almost impossible for Amelia to see in the distance.

At 19.12 hours GMT (7.42 a.m. local time) came a message from Amelia on 3,105kcs, 'KHAQQ calling *Itasca* … We must be on you but couldn't see you, but gas running low … been unable to reach you by radio … we are flying at altitude 1,000ft.' This message came in at strength 5, which was very strong.

Itasca replied immediately at 19.13 (7.43 a.m. local time) with: '*Itasca* to KHAQQ … Received your message signal strength 5 … Go ahead please.' This was followed by a stream of Morse code letter 'A' on frequency 3105kcs and repeated again at 19.17 hours GMT (7.47 a.m. local time). At 19.19 *Itasca* sent another message, '*Itasca* to KHAQQ … Your message okay … please acknowledge with phone on 3105,' followed again by a stream of 'A's in Morse code.

Amelia and Fred were not very confident in the use of Morse code, and for that reason they did not have a Morse key on board. To send any form of short Morse message Amelia would have had to use her microphone button. It appears that Morse code signals to Amelia were only used for the letters A and N, which would have been easy to remember because the letter A was the reverse of the letter N.

A Morse code letter A sounded like 'dit-dah', so a stream would have been /● ▬/● ▬/, which is sounded 'dit-dah/dit-dah/dit-dah/dit-dah'. A Morse code letter N sent sounded 'dah-dit'. Amelia had requested that the USS *Ontario* send out the letter N for five minutes after hour GMT. However, if Amelia had sent out the Morse signals for the letters A or E in a continuous stream on her microphone button it would have helped radio operators to plot the direction of the signals.

The only other signal Amelia would need to use would have been the emergency SOS distress signal (Save Our Souls), which is sounded 'dit-dit-dit, dah-dah-dah, dit-dit-dit'. Sending that signal using her microphone key would have been helpful to alert ships in the area during the final moments before she ran out of fuel. If the aircraft was floating on water, or had even landed on a reef or small strip of land, for a period of time there would have been an opportunity for any radio operators in range to plot the direction of her signals for rescue attempts to be made.

To radio operators the sound of the microphone key being used was known to sound like a generator switching on and off, but with a continuous SOS signal being repeated it would probably have alerted the radiomen to it as being the emergency SOS. There was also the Mayday call that is made over the radio that alerts receiving stations that there is an emergency, but this was not used either.

At 19.29 hours GMT (7.58 a.m. local time) there was a message from Amelia at signal strength 5 (very strong) on 3,105kcs, 'KHAQQ calling *Itasca*. We are circling but cannot hear you. Go ahead on 7,500 either now or on scheduled time on half hour.' Bellarts responded with a long stream of 'A's on 7,500 while they also called by voice. They received an immediate transmission back from Amelia, much to the relief of all who were in the radio room.

At 19.30 hours GMT (8 a.m. local time) there was another message from Amelia, 'KHAQQ calling *Itasca*. We received your signal but unable to get a minimum. Please take a bearing on us and answer 3105 with voice.'

Amelia would have turned the loop aerial of the direction finder to get the Morse code 'dit-dah' 'A' signals repeated over and over, and while turning the loop the A signals should have weakened to the minimum and she then could have got her bearing. It appears that Amelia received very strong 'dit-dah' signals repeated, but on turning loop did not get any point where the signal A volume reduced to a minimum, known as the null, and therefore in her message to *Itasca* she responded, 'unable to get a minimum.'

At 19.35 hours GMT (8.05 a.m. local time) there was a message from *Itasca*, 'Your signals received okay. We are unable to hear you to take a bearing. It is impractical to take a bearing on 3105kcs on your voice … how do you get that … go ahead.'

At 19.36 GMT (8.06 a.m. local time), *Itasca*: 'Go ahead on 3105 or 500 kilo-cycles.'

Itasca had tried to get a bearing on the plane and there had been no response on 7500. It sent a message at 19.42 hours GMT (8.11 a.m. local time), '*Itasca* to KHAQQ … Did you get transmission on 7500kcs? … Go ahead on

500kcs so that we may take a bearing on you … it is impossible to take a bearing on 3105kcs … please acknowledge.'

After repeated messages to KHAQQ with no answer, Bellarts then contacted radioman Frank Cipriani, based in the radio hut on Howland Island, to see if he had picked up anything, but he had not.

In preparation for the landing on Howland Island, a battery-operated high-frequency direction finder had been set up in a hut on the island and was operated by Cipriani. He reported that it was not possible to get any fixes on the plane due to the transmissions being too short. However, by the time the signals were very strong the direction finder had been on so long that the batteries had run down and it would have been impossible to find the direction of the plane. The *Itasca* remained on air sending repeated messages by voice and by Morse code on all frequencies that the plane's radio could receive, but received no answer.

At 20.14 hours GMT (8.44 a.m. local time) Amelia came on air again and was still at strength 5, 'KHAQQ to Itasca … We are on the line of position 157-337 … will repeat this message … we will repeat this message on 6210kcs … wait listening on 6210kcs … we are running north and south.'

Bellarts replied at 20.17 hours GMT (8.47 a.m. local time), '*Itasca* to KHAQQ we heard you okay on 3105 … Please stay on 3105 … Do not hear you on 6210. Maintain QSO on 3105.'

Messages were sent by on both 3105 and 7500 by voice and code, but no further messages were heard from Amelia. He was very concerned because she seemed to be getting stressed, with her voice going to a higher pitch, and also from the hurried way she was delivering her message. Amelia was certainly not her usual cool self and Bellarts commented that 'she was just about ready to break into tears and go into hysterics'.

Itasca continued transmissions for approximately two hours, after which time the captain decided that Amelia had gone down in the sea, so he initiated an immediate search and ordered the *Itasca* to sail for the north-west of Howland Island. It was there that he believed the plane had come down, and with empty fuel tanks it was hoped that it would float for a period of time. It was also very important to try to find the plane before it started to sink, due to the dangers of the shark-infested waters in the Pacific.

George was desperate for news of Amelia. He remembered her fellow aviatrix, Jacqueline Cochran, had previously had psychic visions about some of Amelia's flying activities and contacted her to see if she had had any visions that might help pinpoint where they were. Jacqueline claimed that she had already had a vision that indicated that they were out of fuel and had landed on the water to the north-west of Howland Island. She told George that the plane was floating in the water and although Amelia was not hurt, Fred was unconscious after hitting his head during the landing. She also said that there was a Japanese fishing boat in the area, and gave George the position of where they were. George immediately sent the coordinates to the *Itasca*, which was already steaming to the north-west of Howland Island on the orders of her captain, Commander Thompson. However, once the *Itasca* had arrived at the position given they found that the sea was very rough, with waves up to 6ft, due to the strong wind from the east. These conditions would have been very dangerous for the Electra trying to land on the water. They searched the area very carefully, but no wreckage or sign of survivors in a life raft were found.

The news of the disappearance of Amelia Earhart and Fred Noonan spreads worldwide. (Courtesy of Mary S. Lovell)

7

THE SEARCH

President Roosevelt had been made aware of the disappearance of the Electra and had given instructions that everything possible must be done in the search for Amelia. George contacted Admiral William Leahy, chief of naval operations, for his help, and he then alerted the US Navy Pearl Harbour base in Hawaii to give all assistance possible. The battleship USS *Colorado* had just arrived at Honolulu and was ordered to leave and join in the search, but many of the crew had already disembarked on leave for the 4 July celebrations. They had to be found and told to return to the ship, while at the same time it had to be refuelled and maintenance carried out.

It was thought the plane may have gone down near an island or on a reef and the Phoenix Island area was a possibility due to the islands, especially Gardner Island, being on the line of position 157/337 given by Amelia in her last transmission, when her final words were 'we are running north and south'. The *Colorado* was tasked to search the islands, and once it had arrived in the area its three reconnaissance float planes were catapulted off to fly over Gardner Island (Nikumaroro Island), McKean Island and

Carondelet Reef (Rawaki Island), but nothing was seen other than the remains of a wrecked ship.

Another aerial search was mounted once the alarm had been given, this time with a Consolidated PBY Catalina, which was made ready to fly at 7 p.m. with the aim of arriving in the area by daylight so it could start searching immediately. While on their way, the radioman kept constant transmission, requesting Amelia to press down on her microphone button. He did pick up three dashes, but the crew was not sure if it was from Amelia or from someone else. The Catalina flew into bad weather and the crew received a warning from *Itasca* that the conditions were such that the waves would be too high for them to land on the water and tie up to the ship. With the very poor flying conditions and the possibility of running out of fuel, they decided to return to their base and were not able to join in the search.

The aircraft carrier USS *Lexington*, along with an escort of four destroyers, also joined in the search, and with a squadron comprising sixty-two planes it would be a very useful asset. It was in Santa Barbara, California, and had the same problem as the USS *Colorado*, with many of its crew on 4 July leave who had to be returned to the carrier before it could depart.

It was assumed by the *Itasca's* master, Commander Thompson, that if the plane had been close to Howland it would have seen the island or the *Itasca*, except to the north-west where it was overcast. It was also suggested that if Amelia had not seen Howland Island she may have seen Baker Island, which was just 30 miles to the southeast, but that seemed unlikely as the plane would have been heard or spotted if it had been close to the island. However, Amelia had not indicated that she had seen the island, so Commander Thomson decided that he would focus his search to the overcast north-west of Howland Island as he believed the Electra had come down somewhere beneath the storm clouds in that direction. He immediately ordered his officers and crew to make ready to get underway to search that area.

Later, while the *Itasca* was sailing to the search area, the ship's radiomen picked up a weak voice transmission. They immediately sent a reply, 'You are very weak … repeat … please go ahead,' but there was no reply at first. Then came a second, very weak, voice transmission. The radio team decided to try Morse code and asked, 'If you hear us please give us a series of long dashes.' This was to get an instant response to what appeared to be the on-off of a microphone, which the radioman described as 'like a generator start and stop'. There was a constant stream of weak signals, but many seemed to be false leads. All the information they received was followed up and searched, but nothing was found.

There was an intensive search of the Gilbert Islands, which were 600 miles due west of Howland Island. The minesweeper *Swan* eventually checked out the area and was later joined by the *Itasca*, but no sign of wreckage or survivors was found.

Amelia did not have a Morse code sending key on board and all she could do was use her microphone key. The radiomen were unaware of this, but soon after the sounds were repeated and Bellarts thought he heard a voice saying 'Earhart'. After repeated voice and Morse signals, the next transmission they heard was a man's voice. It was unknown to the radiomen at the time that there was a male navigator aboard, as they thought Amelia was flying solo, so they dismissed the calls.

After the Electra was reported missing there were many hoax messages sent out by people; some of these were taken seriously, causing the *Itasca* to be ordered to search to the south of Howland Island. One woman in Texas, who was tuning her short-wave radio, claimed she heard a very clear message from Amelia, whose voice she said she knew well from listening to her on the radio. The message indicated that the plane was down on an uncharted island, giving the latitude and longitude coordinates of her location, adding that her navigator was seriously injured and needed a doctor. This was not reported to the authorities as the woman thought they were already involved and would have heard the same message.

The Coast Guard was offered the opportunity to broadcast a message on the Hawaiian commercial NBC and KGMB stations. Messages were sent and it waited to see if there was a reply. All stations including navy ships, the *Itasca* and the radio hut on Howland Island were listening in. At 10 p.m. NBC radio sent out a message, 'Amelia Earhart ... if you can hear this signal, please respond on 3105.' At the same time, the Hawaiian Coast Guard Station heard a faint signal, but it was too weak to understand any words.

A short time later, *Itasca* picked up a voice transmission, but was not able to understand the message. The radioman on Howland Island was asked to use the direction finder to find the bearing of the signals, but this could not be obtained. At midnight, a second broadcast was sent out by NBC, but this time the military stations on Hawaii heard a reply, as well as the US Navy, who had also heard a voice. There was again no opportunity to get a bearing. George requested that Honolulu radio station KGU should send out signals asking Amelia to send four long dashes if she heard the message and radio operators immediately heard a response of four long dashes.

At 1.30 a.m. a radio station on Wake Island heard a transmission given with a man's voice, and a listener living just 20 miles from Honolulu picked up a man's voice and heard the call letters KHAQQ as well as 'Help', so he notified the US Navy radio station. Both the Coast Guard on Hawaii and Wake Island radiomen heard the same transmission. Then all went silent.

Other amateur radio stations reported hearing these signals, and some people using the short-wave radios said they heard Amelia's voice and call sign KHAQQ. One report came from a man who had maintained radio contact with Amelia when she made her trans-Pacific solo flight. He claimed that he heard some weak Morse signals on 6210kcs about six hours after her last contact with *Itasca*. The letters he picked up were 'L-A-T' and he thought they may mean latitude. He later claimed to have heard Amelia's voice in a very weak transmission calling, 'SOS, SOS, SOS. KHAQQ, KHAQQ.' However, Amelia's Morse code knowledge was not very strong and it is improbable that she would have known, or have been able to send, the Morse code letters L-A-T. Paul Mantz had commented that it was impossible for the Electra to transmit if floating on the water, as it had no hand-crank mechanism to generate electricity, and the radio could only be used if the engine was ticking over if the Electra had landed on a reef somewhere.

There were also reports that the *Itasca* had seen flares north-east of Howland Island, which it was stipulated could have been distress signals from the plane, but Amelia and Fred had discarded their flares at Lae in their attempt to reduce weight. Astronomers later reported that it was possibly a meteor shower.

Despite such an intense search, nothing was found and on 18 July 1937 President Roosevelt ordered that the search be called off.

THEORIES AND INVESTIGATION INTO THE MYSTERY

Various theories have been given for the disappearance of Amelia and Fred, including those put forward by authors who have conducted specific research studies in an attempt to present their own conclusion to the mystery. These suggested scenarios range from the aircraft being blown off course and crashing into shark-infested waters, to the idea that Amelia was on a government spy mission on the personal orders of President Roosevelt and was captured in Japanese territory and taken prisoner, later dying or being executed. The theory that Roosevelt had sent Amelia on such a mission was summarily dismissed by the First Lady, who said, 'Franklin and I loved Amelia too much to send her to her death.' Furthermore, it was extremely unlikely that Amelia would have agreed to any form of spy mission as she was a firm pacifist; her experiences nursing First World War troops at Spadina would have certainly helped mould her strong views against war.

In 1944, during the Second World War, US Marines landed on the Pacific island of Saipan and claimed to have found a photograph album belonging to Amelia, but that would surely have been an impossibility because she would not have carried any unnecessary weight on the plane. George also travelled there but found no trace of Amelia, and none of the islanders knew about her. Other reports included natives seeing 'a white lady flyer and a man with a bandage on his head', which corroborated with Jacqueline Cochran's psychic vision, although she believed that three days later the plane sank. As part of Jacqueline's work in the Women's Airforce Service Pilots (WASPs) in the war she entered Tokyo just after the surrender but found nothing to explain the disappearance of Amelia, and was left with only her own 'vision' to draw on.

Other potential clues have been found, including messages in bottles washed up on beaches or drifting in the sea, and notes written on pieces of wood supposedly signed by Amelia. The International Group for Historic Aircraft Recovery (TIGHAR) has been active over a number of years and has claimed to have found artefacts that could suggest Amelia ended up on Nikumaroro Island (Gardner Island), which is part of the Phoenix Islands group.

In late 1970, a New Jersey widow and ex-pilot was said to be Amelia living incognito, but the widow denied this rumour and offered to have her fingerprints taken to prove otherwise. In 1960, Fred Goerner, a CBS newsman in San Francisco, began a six-year search, supported by Admiral of the Fleet Chester W. Nimitz, in the belief that Amelia and Fred had died on Saipan. Goerner claimed that US Navy files supported his theory and possibly contained the location of her grave. He did not manage to get these files released to him, but due to the many articles claiming Amelia and Fred had crashed on or near Saipan and were then executed by the Japanese as spies, documents were released in July 1967 to prove otherwise. The official conclusion was that Amelia's plane ran out of fuel about 200 miles north of Howland Island and plunged into the sea.

This was a similar conclusion to the one that Captain Elgen Long and his wife, Marie K., came up with, only they estimated that the Electra was 150 miles closer to Howland Island. The Longs spent more than twenty-five years researching the mystery and wrote the book *Amelia Earhart: The Mystery Solved*, published in 1999 when their 'crash and sink' theory was promoted. This theory concluded that Amelia and Fred ran out of fuel before they could find the tiny Howland Island and were forced to ditch the aeroplane in the ocean. As the Electra was a land plane, it filled with water and sank to the ocean bottom. This theory has been challenged by other researchers, who have drawn their own conclusions, but it should be noted that Long has had a long and distinguished career as a radio operator and navigator on flying boats, including the Boeing 314, and other airliners until he finally retired as a Boeing 747 captain for Flying Tigers. Long was also the first to fly around the world over the North and South poles, where he set fifteen world records and 'firsts'.

Long enlisted in the United States Navy aged 15 and attended both the Aviation Radio and Radar School in San Diego. He served in the South Pacific and first experienced combat missions aged 16. He flew with VP-102 patrol squadron in a PB2Y Coronado flying boat from Canton Island in the Phoenix Islands group, where he learned the basics of celestial navigation. One of his patrol areas was to Baker and Howland Islands, just six years after Amelia and Fred went missing. While flying over Howland Island he could still see the outlines of the runways that had been constructed in 1937 so Amelia could use the island as a refuelling point. These patrol flights were made during daylight and their skills in navigation were based on the same methods used by Fred. With this experience, Long would be better placed to understand the complexities that Amelia and Fred had experienced just six years before.

Clarence S. Williams, a navy navigator, was to prepare the charts in great detail for the whole world route. However, the area that Amelia would fly over in the Pacific Ocean was not well charted and many of them were out of date. The British Admiralty had up-to-date charts but it was not asked for advice, and in February 1937 Williams began to work using the old charts. There had been surveys carried out by the US Navy to correct the old charts and this work had been completed before June 1937, but the new maps were classified, so there was no opportunity for Williams to work from them. This was to be a problem for Fred, as the old charts showed Howland Island to be 6 to 7 miles from its actual position.

Fred was a highly experienced navigator and when they left Lae to fly the 2,556 miles to Howland Island he would have been 90 per cent certain that he would not miss Howland Island by more than 60 miles, owing to the accuracy of his navigation procedures. However, with the out-of-date charts being used that would have created a serious error in the course they were flying. From the evidence reported, it appears that the use of these old charts would have been the most likely reason for the disappearance. It is supported by the fact that the *Itasca,* and those on Howland Island, heard Amelia's voice at strength 5, indicating that the Electra was getting closer. It was believed that they were within 50 to 100 miles of the *Itasca*, but the plane then ran out of fuel and crashed into the sea.

Missions were planned for an underwater search in the waters near Howland Island, where some believe the missing plane is lying on the ocean floor. In 1999, pilot Dana Timmer led searches for the Electra using deepwater sonar. Also involved at the time was Elgen Long and Roy Nesbit, author of the book *Missing: Believed Killed.* The sonar search was working to a depth of 18,000ft below the surface of the water and analysis of the data revealed targets that were approximately the size of the Electra.

Jim Geldert, a naval historian who was also involved as a partner in the 1999 survey, commented, 'We all shared agreement, within miles of the ditching coordinates.' However, Jim continues, 'As a result of recent re-evaluation of original high value targets with much improved sonar/ digital forensics tools, we are planning a return search in the near future.'

AMELIA EARHART'S LEGACY

Amelia Mary Earhart could be described not only as a pioneer for aviation, but also as an activist for equal rights, a pacifist, a teacher, a social worker and an author. She had a shy, charismatic appeal to all who met her, and although often quiet, she had a witty and unique sense of humour. She was was well educated and enjoyed a wide range of interests, especially in music, reading and sports. She was an attractive lady and this was especially apparent when modelling the clothes she designed as part of her display label. But she was most comfortable dressed in her accustomed shirt and trousers with a belt, often a neck scarf, and sometimes even a tie. While one of her reasons for wearing trousers was apparently her dislike of the shape of her ankles, she equally found wearing them much more practical for getting in and out of aircraft.

Amelia was highly independent and courageous, and possessed a steely drive and determination to constantly challenge herself 'to be the first', both in setting records for women and in a desire to beat male achievements in the field of aviation. She believed women should have equal opportunities and not be automatically expected to remain in the home. She wanted women to be able to work in jobs in which they were interested, and she also felt it was essential that they engaged in the right training for these jobs. In this she led by example, taking lessons from a flying instructor to ensure she was competent to fly solo and continuing with relevant training as and when needed to better her pilot skills.

When Purdue University invited Amelia to join the aviation faculty it was an opportunity for her to give lectures that would inspire young women in their own career choices and also enabled her to share her love of aviation. She focused on teaching the girls about recognising their potential and understanding the limits imposed by men and by society, and not allowing this to stop them doing what they want to do.

Amelia helped to form the Ninety-Nines, a non-profit international organisation for women pilots that is still in action today with more than 6,000 members; as well as that, the Amelia Earhart Memorial Scholarship Fund, established in 1939, provides scholarships to aspiring pilots.

It was significant that when Amelia was a social worker she loved her work with immigrant children so much that she fully intended to return to Denison House after the *Friendship* flight was over. Her sister, Muriel Morrissey, later said that she felt Amelia's greatest legacy was probably her ability to provide inspiration for the young.

One of Amelia Earhart's quotes sums up her mindset well and gives an insight into her drive to take up the challenges she set herself throughout her life: 'Never do things others can do and will do if there are things others cannot do or will not do.'

WORLD FLIGHTS

Amelia Mary Earhart's world flight route in 1937: Oakland–Burbank–Tucson–New Orleans–Miami–San Juan–Caripito–Parmaribo–Fortaleza–Natal–South Atlantic crossing–St Louis–Dakar–Gao–Fort Lamy–N'Djamena–El Fasher–Khartoum–Massawa–Assab, Karachi–Calcutta–Akyab–Rangoon–Bangkok–Singapore, Bandung–Surabaya–Kupang–Darwin–Lae. Took off but disappeared before reaching Howland Island. Did not make Honolulu or Oakland.

Her inspiration to aviatrix has been seen by the number of women who have taken up flying, and her attempt to fly around the world has provided a further challenge to others to recreate the flight. However, it must be remembered that the hi-tech navigational equipment and other flying aids used today far exceed those available to Amelia when she made her attempt. For Amelia, the fact she had no co-pilot put added stress on her for the long hours she had to fly, but even for the aviatrix who have taken up that challenge today there have been many hours of flying on each leg, even if they had a co-pilot with whom to share the flying.

There have been serious attempts to recreate Amelia's world flight, led by that of Ann Pellegreno. On 9 June 1967 (thirty years after Amelia and Fred disappeared), Ann left Oakland with her crew of three in a Lockheed 10-A to closely follow Amelia's world flight plan. On 2 July 1967, the same day that Amelia and Fred had planned to arrive there, Ann did a fly-over of Howland Island and dropped a wreath in their memory. The flight continued and they finally landed back at Oakland, California, on 7 July 1967. The flight this time had better refuelling arrangements at various airports and up-to-date radio and navigational equipment. Interestingly, Ann was born the same year as Amelia disappeared on her flight to Howland Island.

Ann's world flight routed Tucson–Fort Worth–New Orleans–Miami–San Juan–Caracas–Trinidad–Paramaribo–Belem–Natal. There was then an Atlantic Ocean crossing to Dakar, with the route continuing Las Palmas–Lisbon–Rome–Ankara–Tehran–Karachi–New Delhi–Calcutta–Bangkok–Singapore–Djakarta–Kupang–Darwin–Port Moresby–Lae. Then came the Pacific Ocean crossing via Nauru and Howland Island, where she did a fly-over before carrying on to Canton Island and Honolulu, and arriving back at Oakland.

Ann's Lockheed 10-A c/n 1112, registration CF-TCA, was originally delivered to Trans-Canada Air Lines and taken on strength in October 1939 by the RCAF as 1526. It was issued to the Flying Instructors School at Camp Borden and was at No. 1 Air Command in January 1945. It was sold to Thunder Bay Airlines in Fort William, Ontario, and then Siple Aircraft of Montreal in July 1946. Later it went to Wisconsin Central Airways, then became an executive transport for Bankers Life and Casualty of Florida before flying on with International Air Services, Lantona State Airlines of Florida and Great Lakes Airmotive of Willow Run, Michigan. It was at Willow Run that the plane was damaged in a belly landing and then sold for scrap. It was rebuilt for Ann's world flight in 1967 and then sold to Air Canada in March 1968. It was first donated to the Museum of Science and Technology and then to the Canada Aeronautical Museum in Rockcliffe with its original TCA registration, CF-TCA.

The next attempt was by Gaby Kennard, who became the first Australian woman to fly a single-engine aeroplane around the world when she left Bankstown, Sydney, Australia, in a Piper Saratoga in 1989, following as closely as possible the flight plan of Amelia and Fred. The flight was made to raise funds for the Royal Flying Doctor Service of Australia, and in recognition for her achievement she was awarded the Harmon Trophy. This award is made annually to the world's outstanding aviator, aviatrix and aeronaut, and was also awarded to Amelia in 1932.

Gaby's flight departed from Sydney's Bankstown Airport on 3 August for Cairns, then on to Port Moresby–Lae–Rabaul–Majuro–Honolulu–Oakland–Winslow–Bartlesville–Memphis–Miami–St Juan–Barbados–Paramaribo–Cayenne–Belem–Fortaleza–Natal–Dakar–Algiers–Agadir–Tunis–Heraklion–Cairo–Luxor–Bahrain–Karachi–Bombay–Madras–Phuket–Singapore–Bali–Darwin–Alice Springs–Parkes. It arrived back at Sydney ninety-nine days later.

Gaby was followed by Linda Finch in 1997, who flew a 1935 restored Electra 10-E on an around-the-world flight to mark the sixtieth anniversary of the disappearance of Amelia and Fred. She left Oakland, California, on 17 March 1997 and after closely following Amelia's route she landed back at Oakland on 28 May. Linda's aim was to share her flight with thousands of children in schools around the world.

Her Lockheed 10-A c/n 1015 was delivered to Northwest Airlines with the registration NC14900. It then went to the United States Army Air Forces and later the Brazilian Air Force, being converted to a 10-E in Brazil. It returned to Northwest Airlines in the USA in 1956.

Linda's world flight route: Oakland–Burbank–Tucson–New Orleans–West Palm Beach–Miami–San Juan–Cumana–Paramaribo–Fontaleza–Natal–St Louis–

Dakar–Gao–N'Djamena–El Fasher–Massawa–Assab–
Karachi– Calcutta–Akyab–Rangoon–Bangkok–Singapore–
Bandung–Surabaya–Kupang–Darwin–Lae–Howland
Island–Honolulu–Oakland.

The fourth flight was by namesake Amelia Rose Earhart,
who was born in 1983 and later became a TV reporter
in Denver. She said she was not related to Amelia Mary
Earhart, but her family shared the same name as the
famous flyer, and she felt fortunate to be named after a
bold courageous woman who had inspired so many parts
of her life. She also became a pilot and, along with her
co-pilot Shane Jordan, took off from Oakland, California,
on 6 June 2014 in a Pilatus PC-12 N58NG to recreate
her namesake's world flight, arriving back at Oakland on
11 July.

Amelia Rose Earhart's world flight route: Oakland–
Denver–Miami–Trinidad and Tobago–Natal–Atlantic
crossing to Dakar–Säo Tomé–Mombasa–Seychelles–
Malé–Singapore–Darwin–Lae–Bonriki–Cassidy
Island–Honolulu–Oakland.

GRACE McGUIRE

Grace McGuire was a small child playing at the side of the
Holy Loch, near Kirn, Scotland, when a seaplane landed
in front of her. This was the first time she had seen an
aeroplane, but even at her young age Grace was very
impressed by it and decided that when she grew up she
wanted to become a pilot.

Her flying lessons started when she was aged 16, but
she was teased by her instructors, who commented that
she was a lookalike of Amelia Earhart. Grace had never
heard of Amelia and became interested in finding out
more about her life.

This became a major turning point for Grace and her studies revealed there had been a number of women who had tried to follow Amelia's 1937 world flight route as closely as possible, but none of them in the original type of Electra 10-E. The 10-E Grace acquired is the only surviving version of the fourteen built of the same model of 10-E that Amelia flew, something that has been verified by the Smithsonian National Air and Space Museum.

The history of the plane starts with 10-E NC14972 c/n 1042 being delivered first to Pan American Supply in December 1935, and from there to Compañía Mexicana de Aviación, registered XA-BJC. In June 1937 it was returned to Pan American World Airways with its original registration. From April 1943 the plane was taken over by Brazilian National Airlines, and in 1956 it was transferred to Provincetown Boston Airways (PBA), where it was used on the Cape Cod–Boston–New York route. In 1970 it was sold to Zepherhills Parachute Centre, Florida, for skydiving operations, and in 1976 it was transferred to Vikings of Denmark Inc. for further use for parachute skydiving by the Raeford Parachute Centre, Raeford, North Carolina. Dolph Overton bought the aircraft in September 1979 and the plane's log records that it was flown to the Wings and Wheels Museum in Orlando, Florida. The plane was eventually stored in the back lot and its condition deteriorated so much that the plan was to cut it up and sell the remains for scrap.

Grace, who had been searching for two years to find the same model plane as Amelia's, heard the museum had a 10-E., commenting:

Christie's auctioned off the contents of the museum and sold Overton's restored Lockheed Electra L-10A (not the same model as Amelia's) to the Science Museum UK. *Muriel* (Lockheed Electra-10-E) was not mentioned in the catalogue and did not sell due to her condition. I went to look at her right after auction but could not buy her as I did not have the funds. I can't remember exactly how long it took to raise the funds but believe I purchased *Muriel* in 1983. UTC President Robert J. Carlson saw me being interviewed on the *Good Morning America* talk show and offered to rebuild *Muriel* and pay for my flight. *Muriel* was trucked to the UTC hangar at Rentschler Field airport in Hartford, Connecticut.

Grace was fortunate to gain the help and expertise of two of Amelia's former mechanics. As she recalled, 'Eddie Gorsky and Ward Oakley were in close touch after I bought *Muriel* and were coaching me on how to rebuild *Muriel*.'

In 1983, Grace was invited to take part in the London–Londonderry air race, and while there she took the opportunity to make a few low passes over the Amelia Earhart monument in the field where she landed on James Gallagher's Farm.

Through the study of original documents, Grace was to discover in the same year that the map and flight plan used by Amelia and Fred, which was prepared by navigator Clarence Williams, had incorrect coordinates for Howland Island that placed them 7 miles (11km) off course. This mistake was based on incorrect charts and would have put the island to the north-west of its actual location.

Unfortunately, Grace was diagnosed with Lyme Disease-induced Multiple Sclerosis shortly after her 1986 expedition to the Howland Island area and her plans for the world flight had to be cancelled. Grace met Amelia Earhart's sister, Grace Muriel Earhart Morrissey, in the

Grace McGuire's *Muriel* in its hangar. (Photograph courtesy of Grace McGuire and Atchison Amelia Earhart Foundation)

Muriel being hoisted on to a flatbed at Gillespie Field airport, San Diego, California. (Photograph courtesy of Grace McGuire and Atchison Amelia Earhart Foundation)

Muriel en route to Tucson, Arizona, for its final destination at Atchison. (Photograph courtesy of Grace McGuire and Atchison Amelia Earhart Foundation)

late 1980s at the Wings Club in New York City, following which the pair became very good friends and travelled a lot together. Muriel died on 2 March 1998 at the age of 98. Grace named her Lockheed 10-E *Muriel* in honour of her friend.

On 15 August 2016, *Muriel* left El Cajon, California, and was escorted through the states of Arizona, New Mexico and parts of Texas to arrive at Atchison on 22 August, where it is being looked after by the Atchison Amelia Earhart Foundation. Grace is now in the process of planning a late 2017 expedition to the area where Amelia and Fred ditched and she will donate anything she finds to the Atchison Amelia Earhart Foundation and the Seaberg family in Atchison.

EPILOGUE

Amelia Earhart is probably the best known aviatrix through-out the world. Even today any mention of her name will elicit a response from most people and there is still a great deal of media interest in her life, career and disappearance.

Despite having an unusual childhood that ricocheted from periods of months, even years, spent with her grand-parents, where Amelia had a comfortable life, to those governed by her father's work as a railroad lawyer, where the family moved from city to city and school to school, she worked consistently at getting herself the best edu-cation possible. Both Amelia and her sister were classic tomboys, not interested in being typical respectable young ladies, but always keen to play all types of games, including those that boys played. Amelia's belief in equality was a long-held one, nurtured during her childhood.

While at her finishing school, Amelia's stubbornness and independence began to show, an attitude that tended to alienate her from her peers and led to her standing her ground against the school staff when she felt she had something important to say. Her drive and determination to learn to fly at whatever cost dictated much of what happened for the rest of her life. Although Amelia became famous after the *Friendship* flight – indeed, a celebrity in the very modern sense of the word, something she found hard to take on board to begin with – she could see that there were challenges to be won in the world of aviation and many more opportunities at achieving 'firsts'. She wanted to be the pilot who succeeded in those milestones. While there were already a number of women pilots who were known to be more skilled than Amelia, she was the one with the backing of George Putnam, whose expertise in the media saw her name constantly appearing in the news, and who was on hand to help 'explain' away any mishap, such as crashes, that she might have.

The theories that have been given for her disappearance have engaged a number of researchers, who have been investigating for many years. They are generally keen to promote their personal accounts of what they have discovered, and heavy speculation is still going on today.

Amelia worked hard and never minded getting her hands dirty, always happy to get stuck in and work alongside the mechanics, who surely enjoyed her joking with them. One of her ex-mechanics was Art Kennedy, who with Jo Ann Ridley wrote the book *High Times Keeping 'em Flying*. In his book, he shares some of the comments that Amelia apparently made to him and his wife, Polly, and revealed that Amelia had asked him not to divulge anything she said. It wasn't until fifty years later when writing his book that he began to disclose the discussions he had had with Amelia. After that length of time, it cannot be easy to recollect with accuracy the details of a specific conversation, or in what context a comment was made – something that could have been intended as a joke, as an aside, or teasing could well be ascribed greater meaning. Nonetheless, some conversations have a greater impact on the memory and are remembered more clearly, even if not word for word, especially when the contents of the conversation were challenging or surprising. However, after a period of fifty years or more, as evidenced from the many interviews I have experienced, even important accounts are not always easy to recollect.

Interestingly, from all the many interactions Amelia must have had with pilots, engineers and friends, there seem to be no other records of any private conversations, such as those written by Art Kennedy, that can be seen to be in any way critical of her lifestyle. She was known to be adept at providing a good 'reason' to explain away any incident or interaction that happened in her life, such as flying accidents and the various other mishaps that occurred during her career. Having said that, surely most of us can be accused of having done something in error and rapidly inventing a plausible excuse to explain ourselves. It is always easy to criticise someone else's actions, especially in retrospect.

Based on the evidence to date, it appears that in her last hours Amelia was close to Howland Island, and by the strength of the radio signals she simply could not have been in the areas that some of the theories surrounding her disappearance indicate. This has been confirmed by a number of experienced navigators who had specific knowledge and skills of the Pacific area where she is thought to have ditched, and searches are continuing even today in these areas.

Further to this, of course, is the crucial evidence of Amelia's final transmissions, during which she was almost hysterical, according to the chief radio operator who took the message. Amelia was usually a cool and unflappable person, calm even when confronted by difficulties, and this extreme stress appears to strongly indicate that she knew they were quickly running out of fuel and would inevitably have to ditch in the sea.

It has since been discovered that the charts they were using were outdated and inaccurate. Amelia's message that they were 'on the line of position 157-337' and they 'were running north and south' indicates that they should have crossed Howland Island if they were going in the correct direction. It is most unlikely that Fred, with his vast experience as a navigator, would have given Amelia the wrong course instructions. One should remember that it was while they were flying across the South Atlantic from Natal to Dakar that Fred instructed Amelia to turn south, but she decided to do the opposite and turn north, as she thought that was the correct course, and they ended up landing in St Louis, Senegal. Had she turned south as advised she would have landed at Dakar in thirty minutes. It would have been unfortunate if she had similarly ignored Fred's course instructions on the Howland flight with fatal results, but, of course, that is just speculation.

Regardless of all the ups and downs that occurred across Amelia's flying career, and whatever the truth of her final journey, there can be no doubt that she was a daring, brave, pioneering and courageous flyer who would take on any challenge that came her way, and she should rightly be remembered for that above all else.

In 1938 Gerard d'Erlanger, Director of British Airways, foresaw that a war with Germany would lead to the cessation of many overseas routes and commercial pilots being left with no planes to fly. He proposed to the British government that there should be a pool of civil pilots that could take over some of the flying assignments undertaken by RAF pilots, such as VIP flights and ferrying aircraft from the manufacturers to the RAF bases, thus allowing the RAF pilots to concentrate on their combat duties. Gerard d'Erlanger was given the job of locating pilots with at least 250 hours' flying time and inviting them for interview for the newly created Air Transport Auxiliary (ATA).

In America, Jacqueline Cochran and Nancy Harkness Love both individually proposed the use of women pilots in the Second World War. Jacqueline also wrote to Eleanor Roosevelt in September 1940 asking for her support for a women's flying division in the air force that could be used for ferrying aircraft from the manufacturing plants to military bases. This would release the male pilots to concentrate on combat duties. However, until an American system was set up Jacqueline and twenty-five other American aviatrix joined the British ATA to ferry aircraft to RAF bases in England.

While Jacqueline was in England, Harkness Love was successful in getting the American Women's Auxiliary Ferrying Squadron (WAFS) started in September 1942. In the meantime, Jacqueline returned from England, and with her experience gained in the ATA she set up the Women's Flying Training Detachment (WFTD) in August 1943.

Both the WAFS and WFTD merged to become the Women Airforce Service Pilots (WASP), with the first graduates emerging in December 1943. However, there was considerable opposition from various quarters, including the press and in Congress, and WASP was finally disbanded in December 1944.

There were also critical comments in the British *Aeroplane Magazine* in 1941, in which C.G. Grey wrote:

There are millions of women in the country who could do useful jobs in war. But the trouble is that so many of them insist on wanting to do jobs which they are quite incapable of doing. The menace is the woman who thinks that she ought to be flying in a high-speed bomber when she really has not the intelligence to scrub the floor of a hospital properly, or who wants to nose around as an Air Raid Warden and yet can't cook her husband's dinner.

One wonders what response Mr Grey would have got from Amelia had she been around at the time and seen the article!

Most of us have memorable dates in our lives, such as birthdays, anniversaries or an event that is important to us. The 2 July 1957 is the date that I will always remember, as that was the day that I joined HM Forces, exactly twenty years after Amelia Earhart and Fred Noonan disappeared in the Pacific Ocean.

Mike Roussel

GLOSSARY

adjustable pitch propeller: A type of propeller with blades that can be rotated around their long axis to change the blade pitch.

airspeed indicator: An instrument used in an aircraft to display speed.

altimeter: An instrument for determining height attained by an aircraft.

autopilot: An automatic system to control the direction, speed and altitude without a human operator being required.

azimuth: The horizontal angle or direction of a compass bearing.

barnstorming: Entertainment given to spectators by stunt pilots where they perform tricks, either on their own or with a group called a flying circus.

barograph: A barometer that records its readings on a moving chart.

bubble octant: A measuring instrument used in navigation.

celestial navigation: Finding directions by observing the sun, moon and stars.

chronometer: A timepiece precise and accurate enough to be used as a portable time standard. It can be used to determine longitude by means of celestial navigation.

compass: An instrument showing the points north, south, east and west and used in navigation.

dead reckoning: The process of calculating position, especially at sea, by estimating the direction and distance travelled rather than by using landmarks or astronomical observations.

drift indicator (heading indicator): A flight instrument that informs the pilot of the aircraft's heading. It is sometimes known as a direction indicator.

great circle route: The shortest distance between two points on the surface of the earth.

ground loop: An uncontrolled turn by an aircraft while taking off or landing that sometime causes one wing to rise and the other wing to touch the ground. This is mainly associated with aircraft that have conventional landing gear, and is due to the centre of gravity being behind the main wheels.

gyroscope: A device used to maintain a directional reference in navigation systems.

loop antenna: A radio device consisting of a loop of tubing.

pelorus: A reference tool for maintaining the bearing of a vessel at sea.

radio bearing: The direction of a radio transmitter from a receiver as determined by a radio direction finder.

radio direction finder (RDF): A device for finding the direction or bearing of a radio source.

BIBLIOGRAPHY

Backus, Jean L., *Letters from Amelia*, Beacon Press, 1982.

Butler, Susan, *East to the Dawn: The Life of Amelia Earhart*, De Capo Press, 1997.

Campbell, Mike, *The Truth at Last*, Sunbury Press, 2012.

Connolly, Sean, *Amelia Earhart (Heinemann Profiles)*, Heinemann Library, 2001.

Earhart, Amelia, *20 Hrs., 40 Min.*, National Geographic Society, 2003.

Earhart, Amelia, *Last Flight*, Orion Books, 1988.

Earhart, Amelia, *The Fun of It*, Academy Chicago Publishers, 1932.

Fleming, Candice, *Amelia Lost*, Schwartz & Wade Books, 2011.

Long, Elmer M. & Marie K., *Amelia Earhart: The Mystery Solved*, Simon and Schuster, 1999.

Lovell, Mary S., *The Sound of Wings*, Hachette Digital, 2009.

Morrissey, Muriel Earhart, *Courage is the Price*, McCormick-Armstrong, 1963.

Morrissey, Muriel Earhart and Osborne, Carol, *Amelia, My Courageous Sister*, Aviation Book Co., 1987.

Nesbit, Roy Conyers, *Missing: Believed Killed*, Pen & Sword Aviation, 2010 revised edition.

Putnam, George, *Soaring Wings*, Harcourt Brace and Company, 1939.

Stone, Lee Tanya, *Amelia Earhart*, DK Publishing, 2007.

INDEX